Navigating Offshore Banking: A Guide for Bank Regulators

Copyright Page

TITLE: Navigating Offshore Banking: A Guide for Bank Regulators

1ST Edition

ISBN: 9798223354970

Table of Contents

Navigating Offshore Banking: A Guide for Bank Regulators

By Roberto Miguel Rodriguez

Chapter 1: Introduction to Offshore Banking

The Concept of Offshore Banking

In the world of finance, offshore banking has become a popular term, often associated with tax havens and financial secrecy. This subchapter aims to provide bank regulators with a comprehensive understanding of offshore banking, its benefits and risks, and its various niches such as offshore banking tax havens, digital nomad tax havens, retirement tax havens, cryptocurrency tax havens, asset protection tax havens, estate planning tax havens, high-net-worth individual tax havens, business tax havens, real estate investment tax havens, and privacy-focused tax havens.

Offshore banking refers to the practice of keeping funds in a bank located outside one's home country. This practice is legal and can offer several advantages, such as tax optimization, asset protection, and privacy. Tax havens, which are countries or jurisdictions with low or no taxes, attract individuals and businesses looking to minimize their tax liabilities. Offshore banking tax havens provide a favorable tax environment, allowing individuals and businesses to legally reduce their tax burdens.

Digital nomads, individuals who work remotely and frequently travel, often seek digital nomad tax havens to benefit from tax advantages and flexible banking services. Retirement tax havens offer attractive retirement packages, including tax benefits and a high standard of living. Cryptocurrency tax havens have emerged as a niche within offshore banking, catering to individuals and companies involved in the digital currency market.

Asset protection tax havens focus on safeguarding assets from legal claims, while estate planning tax havens offer favorable inheritance laws and tax treatments. High-net-worth individual tax havens cater to wealthy individuals, providing specialized banking services and wealth management solutions. Business tax havens attract companies seeking favorable corporate tax rates, business-friendly regulations, and access to international markets.

Real estate investment tax havens offer attractive opportunities for property investors, with favorable tax treatments and potential capital appreciation. Privacy-focused tax havens prioritize financial secrecy and confidentiality, appealing to individuals and organizations seeking to protect their financial information.

While offshore banking provides several benefits, it is crucial for bank regulators to understand the associated risks. These risks include money laundering, tax evasion, and the potential for financial instability if banks face liquidity issues or lack effective regulation.

In conclusion, the concept of offshore banking encompasses a range of niches, each catering to different needs and objectives. Understanding these niches and the associated benefits and risks is essential for bank regulators to develop effective regulations and ensure the integrity of the financial system. By staying informed and adapting to the changing landscape of offshore banking, regulators can strike a balance between facilitating legitimate financial activities and protecting against illicit practices.

The Role of Bank Regulators in Offshore Banking

In the ever-evolving landscape of offshore banking, bank regulators play a crucial role in ensuring the smooth functioning and integrity of these financial institutions. This subchapter explores the significant responsibilities and challenges faced by bank regulators in the context of offshore banking, with a focus on various niche areas such as offshore banking tax havens, digital nomad tax havens, retirement tax havens, cryptocurrency tax havens, asset protection tax havens, estate planning tax havens, high-net-worth individual tax havens, business tax havens, real estate investment tax havens, and privacy-focused tax havens.

Bank regulators act as the primary overseers of offshore banking activities, aiming to maintain stability, transparency, and compliance within these jurisdictions. They are entrusted with the task of enforcing regulatory frameworks, which include licensing and supervising offshore banks, conducting regular audits, and ensuring adherence to anti-money laundering (AML) and counter-terrorism financing (CTF) regulations. By doing so, regulators strive to safeguard the interests of both the offshore banks and the customers they serve.

In the realm of offshore banking tax havens, bank regulators face the challenge of balancing the need for attracting international investors with the risk of becoming a hotspot for illicit financial activities. They must strike a delicate equilibrium, fostering an environment conducive to legitimate business while implementing robust mechanisms to detect and deter money laundering and tax evasion.

Similarly, in the digital nomad tax havens niche, bank regulators must adapt to the unique needs and complexities of individuals who earn income across multiple jurisdictions. They must establish frameworks that facilitate the seamless movement of funds while ensuring compliance with tax regulations in each relevant jurisdiction.

Bank regulators also play a critical role in protecting the interests of retirees who choose offshore banking as a means of preserving and growing their wealth. By enforcing stringent regulations, regulators work towards creating a secure and reliable environment for retirement tax havens, ensuring that retirees can confidently entrust their savings to these jurisdictions.

The rise of cryptocurrencies has introduced a new dimension to offshore banking, with the emergence of cryptocurrency tax havens. Bank regulators must stay abreast of the rapidly evolving crypto landscape, implementing appropriate regulations to mitigate risks associated with money laundering, fraud, and market manipulation.

In conclusion, the role of bank regulators in offshore banking is multifaceted and complex. It requires a deep understanding of the unique characteristics and challenges posed by various niche areas such as offshore banking tax havens, digital nomad tax havens, retirement tax havens, cryptocurrency tax havens, asset protection tax havens, estate planning tax havens, high-net-worth individual tax havens, business tax havens, real estate investment tax havens, and privacy-focused tax havens. By effectively fulfilling their responsibilities, bank regulators contribute to the stability, transparency, and integrity of offshore banking, fostering an environment that attracts legitimate businesses and safeguards the interests of customers.

Benefits and Challenges of Offshore Banking

Offshore banking has gained significant attention in recent years, attracting individuals and businesses alike to explore the numerous benefits it offers. However, it is crucial for bank regulators to understand both the advantages and challenges associated with offshore banking to effectively regulate this sector. This subchapter explores the benefits and challenges of offshore banking in various tax haven niches, including offshore banking tax havens, digital nomad tax havens, retirement tax havens, cryptocurrency tax havens, asset protection tax havens, estate planning tax havens, high-net-worth individual tax havens, business tax havens, real estate investment tax havens, and privacy-focused tax havens.

One of the primary benefits of offshore banking is the potential for tax optimization. Offshore banking tax havens provide individuals and businesses with the opportunity to reduce their tax burdens legally. By taking advantage of favorable tax laws and regulations, individuals can protect their wealth and maximize their profits. This is particularly attractive for digital nomads, as they have the flexibility to work from anywhere and can choose a tax haven that suits their needs.

Retirement tax havens offer retirees the chance to enjoy their golden years while minimizing tax liabilities. These havens often provide tax benefits for pension income, allowing retirees to stretch their retirement savings further. Similarly, high-net-worth individuals can benefit from tax havens that offer favorable tax rates on their investment income and assets, enabling them to preserve their wealth.

Cryptocurrency tax havens have emerged as a popular choice for individuals and businesses involved in the cryptocurrency market. These havens offer a favorable regulatory environment, ensuring privacy, security, and reduced tax obligations for cryptocurrency transactions.

While offshore banking provides numerous benefits, it also poses challenges for bank regulators. One major concern is the potential for money laundering and illicit activities. Bank regulators must implement robust anti-money laundering measures and ensure strict compliance with international regulations to mitigate these risks.

Furthermore, privacy-focused tax havens may impede transparency and hinder the exchange of financial information between countries. Regulators must strike a balance between privacy and the need for transparency to prevent money laundering, tax evasion, and other financial crimes.

In conclusion, offshore banking offers significant advantages for individuals and businesses across various tax haven niches. However, bank regulators must remain vigilant to the challenges associated with offshore banking, such as money laundering and privacy concerns. By implementing effective regulatory measures, bank regulators can create a well-regulated offshore banking sector that fosters economic growth while mitigating risks.

Overview of Offshore Banking Tax Havens

Offshore banking tax havens have long been a topic of interest and scrutiny for bank regulators. These jurisdictions, known for their favorable tax environments and financial secrecy laws, attract various niches such as digital nomads, retirees, cryptocurrency enthusiasts, high-net-worth individuals, businesses, real estate investors, and those seeking privacy-focused financial solutions. This subchapter aims to provide bank regulators with an overview of offshore banking tax havens and their implications for each of these niches.

For digital nomads, offshore banking tax havens offer a range of benefits such as low or zero taxation on foreign-sourced income, flexible banking options, and access to international investment opportunities. These jurisdictions provide a favorable environment for digital nomads to manage their finances and optimize their tax liabilities while working remotely.

Retirement tax havens, on the other hand, cater to individuals seeking to enjoy their golden years in a tax-efficient manner. These jurisdictions often offer retirement-specific incentives, including tax breaks on pension income, exemptions on capital gains, and reduced inheritance taxes. Bank regulators need to understand the nuances of these jurisdictions to ensure compliance and protect the interests of retirees.

Cryptocurrency tax havens have emerged as a new niche within the offshore banking landscape. These jurisdictions recognize and embrace digital currencies, providing a regulated environment for cryptocurrency exchanges, investments, and businesses. Bank regulators must stay abreast of the evolving cryptocurrency landscape to mitigate potential risks associated with money laundering and terrorist financing.

For high-net-worth individuals, asset protection tax havens offer a secure and confidential environment to safeguard their wealth. These jurisdictions provide legal structures such as trusts and foundations that shield assets from litigation, creditors, and inheritance taxes. Bank regulators need to monitor these jurisdictions to ensure proper due diligence and prevent illicit activities.

Estate planning tax havens cater to individuals looking to optimize their estate and succession planning. These jurisdictions offer favorable tax regimes for trusts, wealth transfers, and inheritance taxes. Bank regulators play a crucial role in ensuring transparency and preventing tax evasion within these jurisdictions.

Business tax havens attract companies seeking to establish their headquarters or conduct international trade in a tax-efficient manner. These jurisdictions offer low corporate taxes, tax incentives, and a business-friendly environment. Bank regulators must monitor these jurisdictions to prevent tax abuses and maintain a level playing field.

Real estate investment tax havens provide attractive opportunities for individuals looking to invest in international properties. These jurisdictions offer tax advantages such as exemptions on rental income, reduced property taxes, and favorable capital gains treatment. Bank regulators need to ensure transparency and prevent money laundering risks associated with real estate investments.

Lastly, privacy-focused tax havens cater to individuals seeking financial confidentiality and discretion. These jurisdictions prioritize client privacy and impose strict laws and penalties for unauthorized disclosure of financial information. Bank regulators must strike a balance between privacy and transparency to prevent illicit activities and maintain the integrity of the financial system.

In conclusion, offshore banking tax havens offer unique opportunities and challenges for bank regulators. Understanding the specific needs and risks associated with each niche is crucial to ensure compliance, prevent tax evasion, and maintain the stability of the global financial system. Bank regulators must navigate this complex landscape with diligence and adaptability to protect the interests of both individuals and the wider economy.

Understanding the Importance of Regulation in Offshore Banking

In recent years, offshore banking has gained significant popularity among individuals and businesses seeking financial advantages such as tax savings, asset protection, and privacy. However, the rise of offshore banking tax havens has also brought about concerns regarding money laundering, tax evasion, and other illicit activities. This is where the crucial role of regulation in offshore banking becomes apparent.

For bank regulators, it is essential to understand the importance of regulation in offshore banking to maintain the integrity and stability of the financial system. Offshore banking tax havens, digital nomad tax havens, retirement tax havens, cryptocurrency tax havens, and several other niches within this sector require careful oversight to prevent abuse and ensure compliance with international standards.

One of the key reasons why regulation is vital in offshore banking is to combat money laundering and terrorist financing. By implementing robust anti-money laundering (AML) and know-your-customer (KYC) measures, regulators can prevent illicit funds from entering and circulating within the financial system. This not only protects the reputation of the jurisdiction but also safeguards the global financial system from becoming a safe haven for criminal activities.

Additionally, regulation plays a crucial role in ensuring fair taxation. While tax havens offer attractive tax incentives, it is essential to strike a balance between legitimate tax planning and tax evasion. Regulators must establish clear guidelines and monitor compliance to prevent abuse of these tax advantages. By doing so, they can maintain a level playing field and prevent unfair competition among jurisdictions.

Regulation also helps protect investors and depositors in offshore banks. By imposing capital adequacy requirements and conducting regular audits, regulators can ensure that these banks have sufficient reserves to meet their obligations. This safeguards the interests of depositors and reduces the risk of financial instability.

Furthermore, regulation in offshore banking is essential to maintain transparency and accountability. By requiring regular reporting and disclosure of financial information, regulators can prevent the misuse of offshore structures for illicit purposes. This transparency also enables regulators to identify potential risks and take preventive measures to mitigate them.

In conclusion, understanding the importance of regulation in offshore banking is crucial for bank regulators overseeing various niches such as digital nomad tax havens, retirement tax havens, cryptocurrency tax havens, and more. Effective regulation combats money laundering, ensures fair taxation, protects investors, and promotes transparency. By striking the right balance between facilitating legitimate financial activities and preventing illicit practices, regulators can maintain the integrity of offshore banking and contribute to a robust global financial system.

Chapter 2: Offshore Banking Tax Havens

Definition and Characteristics of Offshore Tax Havens

Offshore tax havens have become a prominent feature of the global financial landscape, attracting various individuals and businesses seeking to minimize their tax liabilities and protect their assets. Defined as jurisdictions with favorable tax regimes, these havens offer unique advantages that cater to the specific needs of different niche groups, including offshore banking tax havens, digital nomad tax havens, retirement tax havens, cryptocurrency tax havens, asset protection tax havens, estate planning tax havens, high-net-worth individual tax havens, business tax havens, real estate investment tax havens, and privacy-focused tax havens.

Offshore tax havens offer several characteristics that distinguish them from regular jurisdictions. First and foremost, they provide a low or zero-tax environment for individuals and entities. This favorable tax regime allows businesses and individuals to legally reduce their tax burdens, thereby maximizing their profits or personal wealth. Additionally, offshore tax havens often have lenient or flexible financial regulations, making it easier for both individuals and businesses to establish accounts and conduct transactions. This flexibility is particularly attractive to digital nomads, who often require quick and seamless access to their funds regardless of their physical location.

Furthermore, offshore tax havens prioritize asset protection and confidentiality. These jurisdictions have strong privacy laws and banking secrecy provisions, safeguarding the identities of account holders and protecting their assets from potential legal disputes or creditors. This characteristic is especially appealing to high-net-worth individuals and businesses seeking to shield their wealth from prying eyes and potential financial risks.

In addition to these general characteristics, specific offshore tax havens cater to niche groups. Retirement tax havens offer favorable tax treatment for retirees, providing them with attractive pension schemes and benefits. Cryptocurrency tax havens, on the other hand, offer a regulatory environment that encourages the growth and adoption of digital currencies, providing benefits such as tax exemptions on cryptocurrency transactions.

Overall, offshore tax havens play a crucial role in the global financial landscape, attracting individuals and businesses from diverse niches. Understanding the definition and characteristics of these tax havens is essential for bank regulators, as they need to navigate and regulate these jurisdictions effectively. By comprehending the unique advantages and challenges presented by offshore tax havens, regulators can develop appropriate policies and frameworks to ensure the integrity and stability of the global financial system while balancing the interests of various stakeholders.

Key Offshore Banking Tax Havens

Offshore banking tax havens have become increasingly popular among various niche groups, including digital nomads, retirees, cryptocurrency enthusiasts, high-net-worth individuals, and businesses seeking to optimize their tax strategies. These havens offer a range of benefits such as favorable tax rates, asset protection, estate planning opportunities, privacy, and attractive investment options. In this subchapter, we will explore some of the key offshore banking tax havens and their unique advantages.

Digital Nomad Tax Havens:

Digital nomads, who work remotely while traveling the world, often seek tax-efficient jurisdictions that allow them to minimize their tax liabilities. Countries like Estonia, where e-residency programs are available, offer tax advantages for nomads, including low corporate tax rates and simplified administrative procedures.

Retirement Tax Havens:

Retirees looking to stretch their retirement savings often consider offshore tax havens that offer lower living costs, favorable tax regimes, and a high standard of living. Popular retirement havens include Panama, Costa Rica, and Portugal, which offer tax incentives for retirees, including exemptions on certain types of income and reduced capital gains tax rates.

Cryptocurrency Tax Havens:

With the rise of cryptocurrencies, individuals and businesses involved in this sector seek offshore tax havens that provide a favorable regulatory environment and tax treatment for digital assets. Jurisdictions like Switzerland, Malta, and Gibraltar have emerged as popular cryptocurrency tax havens, offering clear regulations, tax incentives, and attractive blockchain-related investment opportunities.

Asset Protection Tax Havens:

For individuals and businesses seeking to protect their assets from potential lawsuits or creditor claims, offshore tax havens with robust asset protection laws are highly desirable. The Cayman Islands, British Virgin Islands, and Nevis are known for their strong asset protection frameworks, providing a safe and secure environment for wealth preservation.

Estate Planning Tax Havens:

Offshore tax havens also offer attractive opportunities for estate planning by providing favorable inheritance tax regimes, trust structures, and confidentiality. Countries such as Liechtenstein, Isle of

Man, and Monaco are renowned for their estate planning advantages, allowing individuals to effectively manage and pass on their wealth to future generations.

High-Net-Worth Individual Tax Havens:

High-net-worth individuals seek offshore tax havens that offer a combination of tax advantages, wealth management services, and confidentiality. Switzerland, Singapore, and Luxembourg are known for their strong banking sectors, catering to the needs of affluent individuals and families.

Business Tax Havens:

Businesses often look for tax-efficient jurisdictions that offer low corporate tax rates, ease of doing business, and access to international markets. Countries like Ireland, Hong Kong, and the Netherlands have established themselves as popular business tax havens, attracting multinational companies with their favorable tax regimes and business-friendly environments.

Real Estate Investment Tax Havens:

Investors interested in real estate often turn to offshore tax havens that offer attractive property markets, favorable tax treatment, and potential capital appreciation. Locations such as the Bahamas, Dubai, and Cyprus are known for their real estate investment opportunities and tax advantages for property owners.

Privacy-Focused Tax Havens:

Concerns over privacy and confidentiality drive individuals and businesses to offshore tax havens that prioritize data protection and financial anonymity. Switzerland, the Cayman Islands, and Panama have a long-standing reputation for providing privacy-focused banking services and strict confidentiality laws.

In this subchapter, we have provided an overview of key offshore banking tax havens catering to various niche groups. It is important for bank regulators to stay informed about the evolving landscape of these tax havens to effectively monitor and regulate offshore banking activities.

Cayman Islands

Cayman Islands: A Premier Offshore Banking Destination

Introduction:

The Cayman Islands have emerged as a premier offshore banking destination, offering a wide range of benefits to individuals and businesses alike. As bank regulators, it is crucial to understand the unique features and opportunities presented by this tax haven. In this subchapter, we will explore the various aspects that make the Cayman Islands an attractive option for offshore banking, catering specifically to the niches of the offshore banking tax havens, digital nomad tax havens, retirement tax havens, cryptocurrency tax havens, asset protection tax havens, estate planning tax havens, high-net-worth individual tax havens, business tax havens, real estate investment tax havens, and privacy-focused tax havens.

Overview of the Cayman Islands:

Situated in the Caribbean Sea, the Cayman Islands is a British Overseas Territory known for its political stability, robust financial infrastructure, and favorable tax environment. With a sophisticated legal system based on English common law, the jurisdiction offers a secure and reliable framework for offshore banking activities.

Tax Advantages:

For individuals seeking to minimize their tax liabilities, the Cayman Islands provides an array of tax advantages. With no income tax, capital gains tax, or inheritance tax, it serves as an ideal destination for high-net-worth individuals, retirees, and digital nomads looking to optimize their tax planning strategies. Moreover, businesses can benefit from zero corporate tax, making the jurisdiction an attractive choice for international business operations.

Financial Services:

The Cayman Islands is renowned for its world-class banking and financial services sector. The jurisdiction hosts a multitude of international banks, asset management firms, and trust companies, providing a comprehensive range of services to meet the needs of offshore clients. With a strong emphasis on privacy and confidentiality, the Cayman Islands ensures the protection of client assets and information.

Cryptocurrency and Digital Nomad Opportunities:

As the world embraces digital currencies and remote work, the Cayman Islands has positioned itself as a cryptocurrency and digital nomad tax haven. The jurisdiction offers a supportive regulatory framework for blockchain and cryptocurrency businesses, attracting entrepreneurs and investors looking to capitalize on this rapidly evolving industry. Additionally, with its stunning natural beauty, world-class infrastructure, and favorable tax policies, the Cayman Islands has become an enticing destination for digital nomads seeking a favorable tax environment.

Conclusion:

In conclusion, the Cayman Islands presents an array of opportunities for offshore banking across various niches. Bank regulators must recognize the jurisdiction's appeal to offshore banking tax havens, digital nomad tax havens, retirement tax havens, cryptocurrency tax havens, asset protection tax havens, estate planning tax havens, high-net-worth individual tax havens, business tax havens, real estate investment tax havens, and privacy-focused tax havens. By understanding the unique advantages and regulatory considerations associated with the Cayman Islands, bank regulators can effectively navigate the offshore banking landscape and ensure the integrity and stability of the financial system.

Switzerland

Switzerland: The Quintessential Offshore Banking Tax Haven

Switzerland has long been considered the epitome of offshore banking tax havens. Renowned for its stability, privacy, and robust financial system, this alpine nation has attracted individuals, businesses, and high-net-worth individuals seeking to optimize their financial affairs. As bank regulators, it is crucial for you to understand the unique features and regulations that make Switzerland an attractive destination for various niches within the offshore banking sector.

Offshore banking tax havens have historically been associated with secrecy and non-compliance. However, Switzerland has made significant strides in recent years to align its banking practices with international standards of transparency and regulatory compliance. The Swiss Financial Market Supervisory Authority (FINMA) has implemented stringent regulations, ensuring that the country's banking sector operates with integrity and adheres to global standards.

For digital nomads, Switzerland offers a favorable tax environment. With its low personal income tax rates, individuals can structure their income to benefit from the country's competitive tax regime. Moreover, Switzerland's advanced digital infrastructure and tech-friendly environment make it an ideal location for digital nomads to manage their financial affairs while pursuing their remote work lifestyle.

Retirement tax havens are also plentiful in Switzerland. The country's stable economy, high standard of living, and excellent healthcare system make it an attractive destination for retirees. With a range of tax incentives and retirement savings options, Switzerland offers a secure and comfortable retirement for individuals seeking to protect and grow their wealth.

Switzerland's reputation as a cryptocurrency tax haven has grown tremendously in recent years. The country has embraced blockchain technology and cryptocurrency innovations, creating a favorable regulatory environment for crypto enthusiasts and businesses alike. The Swiss government's progressive approach to digital assets has attracted numerous blockchain startups and cryptocurrency exchanges to set up shop in the country.

Asset protection tax havens are synonymous with Switzerland. The country's robust legal system and strong protection of property rights make it an ideal location for individuals and businesses seeking to shield their assets from potential risks. Swiss banks are renowned for their discretion and provide a safe haven for safeguarding wealth against potential political and economic uncertainties.

Estate planning tax havens also find a home in Switzerland. The country's well-established trust and estate planning laws allow individuals to manage their wealth and ensure a smooth transfer of assets to future generations. Swiss banks and financial institutions offer a wide range of services to assist individuals in preserving and distributing their estates efficiently.

High-net-worth individuals looking for tax-efficient solutions often turn to Switzerland. The country's wealth management industry is renowned for its expertise in catering to the needs of affluent clients. With a vast array of investment opportunities and specialized financial services, Switzerland is a preferred destination for high-net-worth individuals seeking to optimize their tax liabilities.

Business tax havens thrive in Switzerland due to its favorable corporate tax rates and business-friendly environment. The country's stable political climate, skilled workforce, and efficient infrastructure make it an attractive destination for businesses across various sectors. Swiss banks provide tailored financial services to support businesses' growth and ensure compliance with local regulations.

Real estate investment tax havens also have a niche in Switzerland. The country's stable property market, attractive mortgage rates, and favorable tax policies make it an ideal location for real estate investors. From luxury chalets in the Swiss Alps to prime commercial properties in cosmopolitan cities like Zurich and Geneva, Switzerland boasts a diverse range of real estate investment opportunities.

Finally, privacy-focused tax havens find a natural fit in Switzerland. The country's strong privacy laws and strict bank-client confidentiality provisions ensure that individuals' financial affairs remain secure and confidential. Swiss banks are known for their discretion and commitment to safeguarding their clients' privacy, making Switzerland an attractive choice for those seeking to maintain a high level of financial privacy.

In conclusion, Switzerland stands as the quintessential offshore banking tax haven, catering to a diverse range of niches within the offshore banking industry. Its stability, privacy, and robust financial system make it an attractive destination for individuals, businesses, and high-net-worth individuals seeking to optimize their financial affairs.

As bank regulators, it is imperative to stay abreast of Switzerland's unique features and regulations to ensure the integrity and compliance of the offshore banking sector.

Luxembourg

Luxembourg: A Premier Offshore Banking Tax Haven

Luxembourg, a small landlocked country in Western Europe, has established itself as a premier offshore banking tax haven. With its robust financial sector, favorable tax environment, and strict regulations, Luxembourg has become a preferred destination for individuals, businesses, and high-net-worth individuals seeking to optimize their financial affairs.

For bank regulators, understanding the intricacies of Luxembourg's offshore banking landscape is crucial for effective oversight. This subchapter aims to provide a comprehensive overview of Luxembourg as a tax haven, highlighting its unique features and benefits for various niches, including digital nomads, retirees, cryptocurrency enthusiasts, asset protectors, estate planners, and privacy-focused individuals.

Luxembourg's appeal lies in its favorable tax regime, which offers numerous incentives and advantages. The country boasts a low corporate tax rate, making it an attractive destination for businesses seeking to minimize their tax burden. Additionally, Luxembourg's tax treaties with other nations ensure the prevention of double taxation, promoting international cooperation and transparency.

Digital nomads, seeking a tax haven that accommodates their flexible lifestyles, will find Luxembourg's supportive environment appealing. The country's advanced digital infrastructure, coupled with its favorable tax policies, creates a conducive environment for remote workers and entrepreneurs to establish their base.

Retirees also benefit from Luxembourg's tax haven status. The country offers tax advantages for pension income, allowing retirees to safeguard their savings and enjoy a comfortable lifestyle. Furthermore, Luxembourg's high standard of living, excellent healthcare system, and cultural richness make it an ideal retirement destination.

Luxembourg's robust regulatory framework ensures the security and privacy of cryptocurrency enthusiasts. The country has embraced blockchain technology and offers a favorable legal and tax framework for cryptocurrency-related businesses and investors, attracting innovation and fostering the growth of this emerging industry.

Moreover, Luxembourg's asset protection and estate planning solutions provide peace of mind for individuals seeking to safeguard their wealth and plan for the future. Its trust laws, wealth management services, and succession planning options make Luxembourg an attractive choice for high-net-worth individuals and families.

For those concerned about privacy, Luxembourg's commitment to confidentiality and data protection is commendable. Stringent regulations ensure the privacy and security of personal and financial information, making it an appealing destination for individuals who value their privacy.

In conclusion, Luxembourg's position as a premier offshore banking tax haven is well-deserved. With its favorable tax regime, robust regulations, and focus on innovation, Luxembourg offers a wide range of benefits for individuals and businesses across various niches. As bank regulators, a deep understanding of Luxembourg's unique features and advantages will enable effective oversight and ensure the continued success of this thriving offshore banking destination.

Singapore

Singapore: A Thriving Offshore Banking Hub

In the realm of offshore banking tax havens, Singapore stands out as a shining star. This vibrant city-state has established itself as a global financial center, attracting not only high-net-worth individuals but also businesses seeking a favorable tax environment. As bank regulators, it is essential to understand Singapore's unique offerings and its implications for various niche markets, including digital nomads, retirees, cryptocurrency enthusiasts, asset protectors, estate planners, and privacy-focused individuals.

Singapore's appeal as a digital nomad tax haven lies in its robust infrastructure, excellent healthcare, and high standard of living. With its efficient tax system and low personal income tax rates, digital nomads can enjoy the benefits of a well-developed financial ecosystem while minimizing tax burdens. Furthermore, Singapore's digital infrastructure and progressive policies make it an ideal destination for remote workers and entrepreneurs looking for stability and security in their financial transactions.

Retirement tax havens are highly sought after by individuals looking to enjoy their golden years in a financially stable environment. Singapore's strong economy, political stability, and well-regulated financial sector make it an attractive destination for retirees. Additionally, the country offers tempting tax incentives, including the Non-Resident Taxpayer Scheme and the Central Provident Fund, which provide retirees with peace of mind and financial security.

Cryptocurrency tax havens have emerged as a niche market in recent years, and Singapore has positioned itself as a leading player in this space. The city-state has embraced blockchain technology and digital currencies, fostering innovation and attracting cryptocurrency enthusiasts from around the world. Singapore's regulatory framework, which strikes a balance between consumer protection and innovation, has propelled it to the forefront of the cryptocurrency industry.

For those seeking asset protection tax havens, Singapore offers a robust legal framework and a diverse range of wealth management solutions. Its trust laws, strong creditor protection measures, and political stability make it an attractive destination for individuals looking to safeguard their assets from potential risks and uncertainties.

Estate planning tax havens play a crucial role in preserving wealth for future generations. Singapore's well-developed legal system, transparent governance, and efficient probate process make it an ideal choice for individuals seeking to ensure a smooth transfer of assets. The country's trust structures and favorable tax regime provide individuals with the flexibility and peace of mind necessary for effective estate planning.

With its pro-business environment and corporate-friendly tax regime, Singapore has become a sought-after destination for entrepreneurs and high-net-worth individuals. The city-state offers a range of incentives, including attractive tax rates, grants, and subsidies, making it an ideal location for business tax havens. Additionally, Singapore's strategic location, excellent connectivity, and world-class infrastructure make it a gateway to the Asian market.

Real estate investment tax havens have seen a surge in popularity, and Singapore's property market has played a significant role in attracting investors. The city-state offers a stable and robust real estate market, with favorable tax policies and regulations that encourage investment. Its strong legal framework and transparent property market make it an attractive choice for individuals looking to diversify their real estate portfolios.

Privacy-focused tax havens have become increasingly important in an era of heightened privacy concerns. Singapore's commitment to data protection, stringent regulations, and secure banking practices make it an ideal destination for individuals seeking financial privacy. The country's strong legal framework and strict enforcement ensure that privacy-focused individuals can conduct their financial affairs with confidence.

In conclusion, Singapore's status as a thriving offshore banking hub is well-deserved. Its favorable tax environment, robust regulatory framework, and diverse range of financial services make it an attractive destination for various niche markets. As bank regulators, understanding the nuances of Singapore's offerings in offshore banking tax havens is essential for effectively overseeing and regulating this dynamic sector.

British Virgin Islands

The British Virgin Islands (BVI) has long been recognized as one of the premier offshore banking tax havens in the world. Its reputation as a safe and secure financial center attracts a wide range of clients, including digital nomads, retirees, high-net-worth individuals, and businesses seeking to optimize their tax obligations. This subchapter will explore the various aspects of the BVI that make it an attractive destination for offshore banking and discuss its relevance to different niches such as digital nomads, retirees, cryptocurrency enthusiasts, asset protection seekers, estate planners, high-net-worth individuals, business owners, real estate investors, and those in pursuit of privacy-focused solutions.

For digital nomads, the BVI offers a favorable tax environment with no personal income tax, making it an ideal location for professionals who work remotely. Retirees can take advantage of the BVI's tax benefits, including no capital gains tax and inheritance tax, ensuring their savings can stretch further in their golden years.

Cryptocurrency enthusiasts are drawn to the BVI due to its favorable regulatory environment, which has attracted numerous cryptocurrency businesses. The absence of capital gains tax on cryptocurrencies is an added incentive for individuals and businesses involved in this emerging industry.

Asset protection is a crucial consideration for many individuals, and the BVI offers strong asset protection laws. By establishing a trust or company in the BVI, one can safeguard their assets from potential legal claims or creditors.

Estate planning is another area where the BVI shines. Its flexible trust laws and absence of inheritance tax make it an attractive jurisdiction for individuals seeking to protect and pass on their wealth to future generations.

High-net-worth individuals benefit from the BVI's extensive range of financial services, including private banking, wealth management, and trust formation. The jurisdiction's stable political and economic climate, along with its robust legal system, gives these individuals the peace of mind they need to manage their wealth effectively.

Business owners can take advantage of the BVI's tax-neutral environment, which allows for efficient international tax planning and structures. This facilitates global expansion and ensures businesses can operate in a tax-efficient manner.

Real estate investors are attracted to the BVI due to its growing property market and favorable tax treatment of real estate investments. The absence of property taxes and capital gains tax on property sales make the BVI an attractive destination for those seeking to invest in real estate.

Lastly, the BVI is renowned for its commitment to privacy. With strict confidentiality laws in place, individuals can rest assured that their financial affairs remain confidential and protected from prying eyes.

In conclusion, the British Virgin Islands offers a diverse range of benefits for various niches within the offshore banking industry. Its tax advantages, favorable regulatory environment, asset protection laws, and commitment to privacy make it an ideal jurisdiction for individuals and businesses seeking to optimize their financial affairs while ensuring compliance with relevant regulations.

Regulatory Frameworks in Offshore Tax Havens

Introduction:

Offshore tax havens have long been a subject of interest and concern for bank regulators. These jurisdictions, known for their favorable tax laws and financial secrecy, attract a diverse range of individuals and businesses seeking to optimize their financial affairs. This subchapter aims to provide bank regulators with an overview of the regulatory frameworks governing offshore tax havens, as well as the implications for various niches such as digital nomads, retirees, cryptocurrency enthusiasts, high-net-worth individuals, and more.

Understanding Regulatory Frameworks:

Regulatory frameworks in offshore tax havens are designed to strike a delicate balance between attracting international capital and ensuring compliance with global standards. These frameworks typically comprise legislation, regulations, and supervisory mechanisms that govern the operations of financial institutions, including banks, investment funds, and insurance companies.

Key Components of Regulatory Frameworks:

1. Anti-Money Laundering (AML) and Know Your Customer (KYC) Measures: Offshore tax havens have increasingly strengthened their AML and KYC requirements to combat money laundering, terrorist financing, and other illicit activities. Bank regulators play a crucial role

in ensuring that financial institutions comply with these measures and maintain robust due diligence practices.

2. Tax Transparency and Exchange of Information: In recent years, offshore tax havens have faced mounting pressure to improve tax transparency and facilitate the exchange of relevant financial information with other jurisdictions. Bank regulators must monitor compliance with international standards, such as the Common Reporting Standard (CRS) and Foreign Account Tax Compliance Act (FATCA), to ensure the integrity of their respective tax systems.

Implications for Various Niches:

1. Digital Nomad Tax Havens: Bank regulators should consider the unique challenges posed by digital nomads, who often rely on offshore tax havens for their flexible work arrangements. Ensuring compliance with tax obligations and addressing potential abuses of residency requirements are key areas of focus.

2. Retirement Tax Havens: Bank regulators need to ensure that offshore retirement destinations provide adequate consumer protection for retirees, including secure pension schemes and transparent investment options.

3. Cryptocurrency Tax Havens: As cryptocurrencies gain popularity, bank regulators must address the regulatory challenges associated with their use in offshore tax havens. This includes establishing frameworks for the licensing and supervision of cryptocurrency exchanges and custodial services.

Conclusion:

Regulatory frameworks in offshore tax havens are constantly evolving in response to global initiatives aimed at combating tax evasion, money laundering, and other financial crimes. Bank regulators have a crucial role to play in ensuring that these jurisdictions strike the right balance between attracting international capital and maintaining the integrity of their financial systems. By staying abreast of the latest developments, regulators can effectively navigate the complexities of offshore tax havens and safeguard the interests of stakeholders across a range of niches, from digital nomads to high-net-worth individuals and business owners.

Anti-Money Laundering (AML) Regulations

In the world of offshore banking, the issue of money laundering has become a critical concern. As bank regulators, it is essential for you to understand and enforce Anti-Money Laundering (AML) regulations to maintain the integrity of the financial system. This subchapter will provide an overview of AML regulations and their significance in various niches of offshore banking.

Offshore banking tax havens, digital nomad tax havens, retirement tax havens, cryptocurrency tax havens, asset protection tax havens, estate planning tax havens, high-net-worth individual tax havens, business tax havens, real estate investment tax havens, and privacy-focused tax havens all share a common need for robust AML regulations. These regulations are designed to prevent illicit funds from entering the financial system, protect investors, and maintain the reputation of tax havens as secure and reliable banking jurisdictions.

AML regulations require financial institutions in tax havens to implement rigorous due diligence procedures when onboarding clients. This includes verifying the identity of individuals and businesses, assessing the source of funds, and monitoring transactions for suspicious activities. By adhering to these regulations, tax havens can ensure that only legitimate funds flow through their banking systems, thereby mitigating the risk of money laundering.

In the realm of digital nomad tax havens and cryptocurrency tax havens, AML regulations play a crucial role in preventing the misuse of decentralized digital currencies. These regulations require businesses operating in these tax havens to implement robust know-your-customer (KYC) procedures and report any suspicious transactions to the relevant authorities. By doing so, these tax havens can strike a balance between embracing innovative financial technologies and maintaining regulatory compliance.

Furthermore, AML regulations are of utmost importance in asset protection tax havens, estate planning tax havens, and high-net-worth individual tax havens. These niches attract individuals and families looking to safeguard their wealth and assets. AML regulations ensure that these tax havens do not become safe havens for criminals seeking to launder illicit funds. By enforcing stringent due diligence and transaction monitoring measures, these tax havens can maintain their credibility as secure jurisdictions for asset protection and estate planning purposes.

In conclusion, AML regulations are a vital component of offshore banking in various tax haven niches. Bank regulators must understand and enforce these regulations to safeguard the financial system, protect investors, and maintain the reputation of tax havens. By doing so, offshore banking tax havens, digital nomad tax havens, retirement tax havens, cryptocurrency tax havens, asset protection tax havens, estate planning tax havens, high-net-worth individual tax havens, business tax havens, real estate investment tax havens, privacy-focused tax havens can continue to thrive as trusted and reliable financial jurisdictions.

Know Your Customer (KYC) Requirements

In today's rapidly evolving banking landscape, it is paramount for bank regulators to have a thorough understanding of the Know Your Customer (KYC) requirements. KYC is a fundamental process that banks and financial institutions use to verify the identity of their customers and assess their suitability for different banking services. This subchapter will delve into the significance of KYC requirements and their implications for various niches in the offshore banking industry.

Offshore banking tax havens, digital nomad tax havens, retirement tax havens, cryptocurrency tax havens, asset protection tax havens, estate planning tax havens, high-net-worth individual tax havens, business tax havens, real estate investment tax havens, and privacy-focused tax havens all have unique characteristics, but they share the common need for robust KYC procedures.

The KYC process involves collecting and verifying customer information, including their identity, address, occupation, and source of funds. Bank regulators must understand the importance of KYC requirements to prevent money laundering, terrorist financing, tax evasion, and other illicit activities that can occur in these offshore banking jurisdictions.

For offshore banking tax havens, KYC requirements are crucial to maintain the integrity of the jurisdiction and ensure compliance with international standards. By implementing stringent KYC procedures, bank regulators can mitigate the risk of offshore banking becoming a safe haven for money laundering and illicit financial activities.

In the case of digital nomad tax havens, KYC requirements play a vital role in verifying the legitimacy of individuals claiming residency in these jurisdictions. Effective KYC measures ensure that digital nomads are genuine residents and not using tax havens as a means to evade taxes in their home countries.

Similarly, retirement tax havens, cryptocurrency tax havens, asset protection tax havens, estate planning tax havens, high-net-worth individual tax havens, business tax havens, real estate investment tax havens, and privacy-focused tax havens all benefit from robust KYC requirements. These measures help safeguard the reputation of these jurisdictions, attract legitimate investors, and deter individuals seeking to exploit them for illicit purposes.

Bank regulators must continually update and enforce KYC requirements to keep pace with evolving financial crimes and technologies. They should collaborate with international organizations, share information with other jurisdictions, and stay informed about emerging risks and best practices in KYC procedures.

In conclusion, understanding and implementing effective KYC requirements is of utmost importance for bank regulators in offshore banking tax havens, digital nomad tax havens, retirement tax havens, cryptocurrency tax havens, asset protection tax havens, estate planning tax havens, high-net-worth individual tax havens, business tax havens, real estate investment tax havens, and privacy-focused tax havens. By doing so, they can ensure the integrity, security, and compliance of the offshore banking industry while fostering legitimate economic growth.

Reporting and Transparency Standards

In today's globalized economy, offshore banking tax havens have become increasingly popular among various niches, including digital nomads, retirees, cryptocurrency enthusiasts, high-net-worth individuals, and business owners. These jurisdictions offer unique advantages such as reduced tax burdens, asset protection, and privacy-focused services. However, with the growth of offshore banking, there is a need for robust reporting and transparency standards to ensure the integrity of these tax havens and protect the interests of both regulators and clients.

Bank regulators play a crucial role in establishing and enforcing reporting and transparency standards in offshore banking tax havens. These standards aim to enhance the credibility of these jurisdictions by ensuring that financial institutions operating within them adhere to internationally accepted practices. By doing so, bank regulators can foster trust, attract foreign investment, and prevent illicit activities such as money laundering and tax evasion.

One key aspect of reporting and transparency standards is the requirement for financial institutions to provide accurate and timely information to regulatory authorities. This includes detailed reports on their clients, assets under management, and any suspicious transactions. Regulators should establish clear guidelines on what information needs to be disclosed and set strict deadlines to ensure compliance.

Furthermore, bank regulators should collaborate with international bodies such as the Financial Action Task Force (FATF) and the Organisation for Economic Co-operation and Development (OECD) to align reporting and transparency standards with global best practices. By adopting internationally recognized standards, offshore banking tax havens can demonstrate their commitment to combating financial crime and avoiding being labeled as non-cooperative jurisdictions.

To facilitate effective reporting, regulators should encourage the use of digital platforms and technologies that enable secure and efficient data exchange between financial institutions and regulatory authorities. The implementation of robust reporting systems can help regulators collect and analyze data effectively, identify potential risks, and take appropriate actions promptly.

Transparency is another crucial element in ensuring the integrity of offshore banking tax havens. Regulators should require financial institutions to disclose their ownership structure, beneficial owners, and key personnel. This information should be easily accessible to regulators and clients to promote accountability and deter illicit activities.

In conclusion, reporting and transparency standards are vital for the sustainable development of offshore banking tax havens. Bank regulators have a crucial role in establishing and enforcing these standards to ensure the integrity of these jurisdictions and protect the interests of clients. By adopting internationally recognized practices, implementing robust reporting systems, and promoting transparency, offshore banking tax havens can maintain their reputation as credible and trustworthy financial centers.

Chapter 3: Digital Nomad Tax Havens

Understanding the Concept of Digital Nomads

In recent years, the rise of digital nomads has revolutionized the way people work and live. These individuals, often referred to as location-independent professionals, have embraced a lifestyle that allows them to work remotely and travel the world while earning an income. As bank regulators, it is crucial to understand the concept of digital nomads and the implications they have on offshore banking and tax havens.

Digital nomads are individuals who leverage technology to work remotely, freeing themselves from the constraints of a traditional office environment. They rely on laptops, smartphones, and an internet connection to carry out their work, allowing them the flexibility to work from any location they desire. This newfound freedom has led to a surge in the number of people choosing to become digital nomads, seeking tax havens and offshore banking solutions that align with their lifestyle.

For offshore banking tax havens, digital nomads pose unique challenges and opportunities. These individuals often have complex financial situations, with income derived from various sources across different jurisdictions. Regulators must understand the specific needs and requirements of digital nomads to ensure that offshore banking services cater to their financial needs while complying with relevant regulations.

Digital nomads also have distinct tax considerations. Many countries have introduced special tax regimes to attract these individuals, offering advantages such as lower tax rates or exemptions on foreign-sourced income. Regulators must be well-versed in the tax laws and regulations of these jurisdictions to effectively oversee offshore banking services provided to digital nomads.

Furthermore, digital nomads have specific demands when it comes to asset protection, estate planning, and privacy-focused banking. Bank regulators need to ensure that offshore banking institutions are equipped to handle these requirements, providing appropriate services and safeguards to protect the assets and privacy of digital nomads.

Additionally, the rise of cryptocurrencies has further complicated the landscape for digital nomads and offshore banking tax havens. As more digital nomads embrace cryptocurrencies as a means of transacting and preserving wealth, regulators must keep pace with the evolving regulatory frameworks surrounding cryptocurrencies to mitigate risks and ensure compliance.

Understanding the concept of digital nomads is crucial for bank regulators in navigating the offshore banking landscape. By acknowledging the unique needs and challenges faced by digital nomads, regulators can develop effective policies and regulations that facilitate the provision of offshore banking services to this growing niche.

Popular Digital Nomad Tax Havens

As the digital nomad lifestyle continues to gain popularity, more individuals are seeking out tax havens that cater specifically to their unique needs. These tax havens offer favorable tax regimes and a welcoming environment for remote workers who travel the world while earning an income. In this subchapter, we will explore some of the most popular digital nomad tax havens and the benefits they offer.

One of the top digital nomad tax havens is Estonia. Known for its progressive digital infrastructure, Estonia offers a unique e-Residency program that allows individuals to establish and operate a location-independent business. Digital nomads can take advantage of Estonia's favorable tax system, which includes a flat corporate tax rate of 20% and a simplified tax reporting process.

Another popular choice for digital nomads is Portugal. With its attractive tax system, which includes a Non-Habitual Resident (NHR) regime, Portugal offers significant tax benefits to foreign residents. Under the NHR regime, qualifying individuals can be exempt from income tax on foreign-sourced income for a period of 10 years. This makes Portugal an ideal tax haven for digital nomads who earn income from clients or businesses outside the country.

For those seeking a tropical paradise, the Cayman Islands is a popular destination. With no income, capital gains, or corporate taxes, the Cayman Islands offers a tax-friendly environment for digital nomads. Additionally, the Cayman Islands is well-regarded for its strong financial services sector and robust legal framework, making it an attractive jurisdiction for offshore banking and asset protection.

Singapore is another tax haven that appeals to digital nomads. Known for its low personal and corporate tax rates, Singapore offers a competitive tax environment for both individuals and businesses. Additionally, Singapore is renowned for its efficient regulatory system and strong rule of law, making it an ideal jurisdiction for offshore banking and cryptocurrency investments.

These are just a few examples of the popular digital nomad tax havens available for remote workers. Each tax haven offers its own unique set of benefits, from favorable tax rates to strong legal frameworks. As bank regulators, it is important to understand the specific needs and challenges faced by digital nomads, and to ensure that their financial transactions and investments are conducted in compliance with applicable regulations.

By providing a regulatory framework that supports the digital nomad lifestyle and offshore banking, bank regulators can foster an environment that attracts and retains this growing niche of individuals. In doing so, they can contribute to the economic growth and development of these tax havens while ensuring the integrity of the global financial system.

Estonia

Estonia: A Progressive Approach to Offshore Banking and Tax Havens

Estonia, a small Baltic nation known for its technological advancements and forward-thinking policies, has emerged as a prominent player in the world of offshore banking and tax havens. With a robust regulatory framework and attractive incentives, Estonia offers a unique and favorable environment for individuals and businesses seeking to optimize their financial affairs.

For bank regulators, understanding Estonia's approach to offshore banking is crucial in effectively monitoring and ensuring compliance with international standards. This subchapter aims to provide an overview of Estonia's offshore banking landscape, focusing on its relevance to various niches within the industry.

Digital nomads, a growing segment of the global workforce, are drawn to Estonia's e-Residency program, which allows them to establish and manage their businesses remotely. By leveraging the country's advanced digital infrastructure and favorable tax policies, digital nomads can enjoy the benefits of offshore banking while maintaining flexibility and mobility.

Retirement tax havens have long been sought after by individuals looking to secure their financial future. Estonia's pension system, characterized by a transparent and efficient framework, offers great opportunities for retirees to optimize their savings and benefit from favorable tax treatment.

Cryptocurrency tax havens have gained significant attention in recent years, and Estonia has positioned itself as a leader in this space. With a progressive approach to blockchain technology and a supportive regulatory environment, Estonia has become an attractive destination for cryptocurrency businesses and investors.

For those seeking asset protection, estate planning, or privacy-focused solutions, Estonia offers a range of options. Its strong legal framework, including the use of digital signatures and encrypted communication, provides individuals and businesses with enhanced privacy and security.

High-net-worth individuals, business owners, and real estate investors also find Estonia appealing due to its competitive tax rates, ease of doing business, and stable economy. By establishing a presence in Estonia, they can take advantage of the country's favorable tax regime and benefit from its strategic location within the European Union.

In conclusion, Estonia's progressive approach to offshore banking and tax havens has positioned it as a leading destination for individuals and businesses seeking to optimize their financial affairs. Bank regulators must familiarize themselves with Estonia's unique offerings and adapt their strategies to effectively monitor and regulate this dynamic sector. By doing so, they can ensure that Estonia continues to thrive as a reliable and responsible player in the offshore banking industry.

Portugal

Portugal: An Emerging Offshore Banking Destination

In recent years, Portugal has emerged as a prominent player in the offshore banking industry, attracting a diverse range of individuals and businesses seeking tax advantages and financial privacy. With its strategic location, attractive tax incentives, and stable economy, Portugal has become an ideal destination for those looking to optimize their financial strategies.

For bank regulators monitoring the offshore banking sector, understanding the dynamics of Portugal's offshore banking system is crucial. This subchapter aims to provide an overview of Portugal as an offshore banking tax haven and its appeal to various niche groups such as digital nomads, retirees, cryptocurrency enthusiasts, high-net-worth individuals, businesses, real estate investors, and privacy-focused individuals.

Portugal offers several advantages as an offshore banking tax haven. Firstly, it provides a territorial tax system, wherein only income generated within Portugal is subject to taxation. This makes it an attractive option for digital nomads and remote workers who can benefit from Portugal's Non-Habitual Resident (NHR) program. Under this regime, individuals can enjoy a flat income tax rate of 20% for qualifying income streams for ten years, making it one of the most attractive tax havens for this niche.

Retirees also flock to Portugal due to its generous tax incentives and high quality of life. The Non-Habitual Resident (NHR) program mentioned earlier also applies to retirees, offering a 10-year tax exemption on certain foreign incomes. Moreover, Portugal's Golden Visa program provides residency permits to non-European Union individuals investing in real estate, making it an enticing option for those seeking a retirement tax haven.

Portugal's friendly stance towards cryptocurrencies has made it a sought-after destination for cryptocurrency enthusiasts and investors. The country has implemented a progressive regulatory framework, offering clarity and security for cryptocurrency businesses.

Furthermore, income from cryptocurrency transactions is tax-free for individuals, further solidifying Portugal's position as a cryptocurrency tax haven.

High-net-worth individuals find Portugal appealing due to its favorable tax regime for wealth and inheritance. The Non-Habitual Resident (NHR) program exempts income from foreign sources, including inheritances, from taxation. Additionally, Portugal does not impose wealth or gift taxes, making it an attractive option for estate planning and asset protection.

Businesses also find Portugal's tax regime favorable. The country offers a competitive corporate tax rate of 21%, making it an attractive destination for entrepreneurs and corporations looking for business tax havens. Furthermore, Portugal boasts a skilled workforce, excellent infrastructure, and access to the European market, making it an ideal location for companies to establish their presence.

Real estate investment tax havens are also of interest in Portugal. The Golden Visa program mentioned earlier not only applies to retirees but also encourages real estate investment. This program provides a path to Portuguese citizenship for individuals investing in the country's real estate market, making it an appealing option for real estate investors seeking tax advantages.

Lastly, Portugal's commitment to privacy-focused individuals cannot be overlooked. The country has implemented robust privacy laws, ensuring the confidentiality of banking and financial transactions. Combined with its stable political and economic environment, Portugal has become a preferred choice for individuals seeking privacy-focused tax havens.

In conclusion, Portugal has emerged as a compelling offshore banking destination offering various tax advantages and financial opportunities for different niche groups. For bank regulators, understanding the intricacies of Portugal's offshore banking system is vital in ensuring compliance and monitoring the ever-evolving landscape of offshore banking tax havens.

Thailand

Thailand: A Prominent Offshore Banking and Tax Haven

Thailand has emerged as a prominent player in the world of offshore banking and tax havens, attracting a diverse range of individuals and businesses seeking favorable financial environments. Bank regulators must understand the nuances of Thailand's offshore banking sector to effectively navigate its regulatory landscape and ensure compliance.

Offshore banking tax havens: Thailand offers a range of tax incentives and a favorable regulatory framework for offshore banking activities. The country's robust financial infrastructure and stable political environment make it an attractive destination for individuals and businesses looking to optimize their tax liabilities.

Digital nomad tax havens: Thailand's affordable cost of living, vibrant digital nomad community, and progressive visa policies have made it a popular choice for location-independent professionals. Bank regulators must understand the unique banking needs of digital nomads and ensure that appropriate regulations are in place to support their financial activities.

Retirement tax havens: With its beautiful landscapes, affordable healthcare, and friendly culture, Thailand has become a sought-after retirement destination. Bank regulators must be aware of the specific financial requirements and challenges faced by retirees and create a regulatory environment that encourages secure and efficient banking services for this niche.

Cryptocurrency tax havens: Thailand has been proactive in regulating the cryptocurrency industry, offering clarity and certainty to businesses involved in this sector. Bank regulators must stay updated on the evolving landscape of cryptocurrencies and create frameworks that promote responsible and secure banking practices.

Asset protection tax havens: Thailand's strong legal framework and asset protection laws make it an attractive destination for individuals and businesses looking to safeguard their assets. Bank regulators must ensure that appropriate oversight is in place to prevent money laundering and other illicit activities while allowing for legitimate asset protection strategies.

Estate planning tax havens: Thailand's favorable inheritance laws and tax regime make it an ideal location for estate planning purposes. Bank regulators must understand the intricacies of estate planning and collaborate with legal authorities to ensure that the banking sector supports efficient and transparent transfer of wealth.

High-net-worth individual tax havens: Thailand's banking sector offers a range of services tailored to high-net-worth individuals, including private banking, wealth management, and investment advisory. Bank regulators must ensure that these services are provided with the highest standards of transparency and compliance.

Business tax havens: Thailand's pro-business policies, low taxes, and skilled workforce have attracted numerous businesses to set up operations in the country. Bank regulators must create an environment that fosters responsible banking practices and supports the growth of businesses while preventing money laundering and other financial crimes.

Real estate investment tax havens: Thailand's thriving real estate market and favorable investment laws have made it a popular destination for property investors. Bank regulators must monitor real estate transactions to prevent money laundering and ensure that the banking sector supports transparent and secure property investments.

Privacy-focused tax havens: Thailand's banking sector is known for its commitment to client privacy and confidentiality. Bank regulators must strike a balance between privacy and the need to prevent financial crimes, ensuring that appropriate regulations are in place to protect client information while enforcing anti-money laundering measures.

In summary, Thailand offers a diverse range of opportunities for offshore banking and tax planning across various niches. Bank regulators must stay updated on the unique requirements and challenges of each niche to effectively navigate Thailand's regulatory landscape and ensure a secure and compliant offshore banking environment.

Costa Rica

Costa Rica: A Haven for Offshore Banking and Tax Planning

Costa Rica, a small Central American country known for its stunning natural beauty, has emerged as a popular destination for offshore banking and tax planning. With its stable political climate, robust financial sector, and attractive tax incentives, Costa Rica offers a range of benefits for individuals and businesses seeking financial privacy and tax optimization.

For offshore banking tax havens, Costa Rica has positioned itself as a prime choice. The country boasts a well-regulated banking system, with a strong emphasis on client confidentiality. Bank regulators can rest assured that their clients' assets will be protected, as Costa Rica maintains strict banking secrecy laws, making it an ideal jurisdiction for safeguarding wealth.

Digital nomads, a growing niche of individuals who work remotely while traveling, can also find Costa Rica to be a tax haven. The country offers a territorial tax system, which means that income generated outside of Costa Rica is not subject to local taxation. This attractive tax structure allows digital nomads to enjoy the benefits of a tropical paradise while minimizing their tax liabilities.

Retirement tax havens are another niche that Costa Rica caters to. The country offers a range of incentives for retirees, including a generous pensionado program, which grants tax exemptions on income derived from outside of Costa Rica. Retirees can take advantage of Costa Rica's affordable cost of living, stunning landscapes, and excellent healthcare system while enjoying favorable tax treatment.

In recent years, Costa Rica has also gained traction as a cryptocurrency tax haven. The country has embraced digital currencies and blockchain technology, attracting cryptocurrency investors and entrepreneurs. With its favorable regulatory environment and low tax rates, Costa Rica provides a secure and tax-efficient ecosystem for the cryptocurrency industry to thrive.

Additionally, Costa Rica serves as a hub for asset protection and estate planning tax havens. The country offers a range of legal structures, such as trusts and foundations, which allow individuals to protect their assets and plan for the orderly transfer of wealth. Bank regulators can confidently recommend Costa Rica as a jurisdiction that provides robust asset protection mechanisms and favorable estate planning opportunities.

High-net-worth individuals, businesses, and real estate investors can also benefit from Costa Rica's business and real estate investment tax havens. With its attractive tax incentives, low corporate tax rates, and a welcoming business environment, Costa Rica has become an attractive destination for entrepreneurs and investors. Furthermore, the booming real estate market offers lucrative investment opportunities, with tax advantages for those looking to diversify their portfolios.

Lastly, Costa Rica stands out as a privacy-focused tax haven. The country respects individuals' privacy and confidentiality, making it an attractive choice for those seeking to protect their financial information. Costa Rica's commitment to privacy and its robust legal framework ensure that bank regulators can confidently recommend the country as a jurisdiction that values and protects privacy.

In conclusion, Costa Rica offers a myriad of benefits for bank regulators and their clients across various niches of offshore banking and tax planning. With its stable political environment, strong financial sector, attractive tax incentives, and commitment to privacy, Costa Rica has positioned itself as a leading destination for individuals and businesses seeking financial optimization and asset protection.

Malta

Malta: A Versatile Tax Haven for Offshore Banking

Located in the heart of the Mediterranean, Malta is a small but significant player in the world of offshore banking. With its favorable tax laws, robust regulatory framework, and strategic location, this island nation has emerged as a popular choice for individuals and businesses seeking to optimize their financial affairs.

For bank regulators, understanding Malta's unique position as an offshore banking tax haven is crucial. Malta offers a range of attractive features that cater to various niches, including digital nomads, retirees, cryptocurrency enthusiasts, high-net-worth individuals, and businesses.

One of Malta's key strengths is its tax regime. The country has a competitive corporate tax rate of 35%, which can be reduced to as low as 5% through various incentives and structures. This makes it an ideal destination for businesses looking to establish a presence in a tax-efficient jurisdiction. Additionally, Malta does not impose capital gains taxes on most types of investments, making it an attractive option for real estate investors and those seeking asset protection.

Malta's regulatory environment is also worth noting. The country has a well-established financial services authority that ensures compliance with international standards, such as anti-money laundering (AML) and know-your-customer (KYC) regulations. This provides bank regulators with confidence that offshore banking activities in Malta are conducted in a secure and transparent manner.

Furthermore, Malta has embraced the digital revolution, positioning itself as a leading jurisdiction for cryptocurrency and blockchain-related activities. The government has introduced a comprehensive regulatory framework for virtual financial assets, offering clarity and legal certainty to businesses and individuals operating in this space. This has attracted a growing number of cryptocurrency enthusiasts and businesses seeking a privacy-focused tax haven.

In addition to its favorable tax and regulatory environment, Malta boasts a high quality of life, making it an appealing option for retirees and digital nomads. The island offers a pleasant climate, a low crime rate, and a vibrant cultural scene. English is widely spoken, making it easy for expatriates to integrate into the local community.

Overall, Malta offers a versatile range of benefits for bank regulators and individuals alike. As a tax haven, it caters to multiple niches, including offshore banking, digital nomadism, retirement, cryptocurrency, asset protection, estate planning, high-net-worth individuals, business, real estate investment, and privacy-focused individuals. By understanding the nuances of Malta's tax and regulatory landscape, bank regulators can effectively navigate the world of offshore banking and ensure compliance with international standards.

Tax Benefits and Considerations for Digital Nomads

As the world becomes increasingly interconnected, a growing number of individuals are embracing the digital nomad lifestyle. These adventurous souls leverage technology to work remotely while exploring new destinations around the globe. With this rise in digital nomadism comes the need for a deeper understanding of the tax implications and benefits that exist for this unique group of individuals.

For bank regulators overseeing offshore banking tax havens, it is crucial to recognize the potential for digital nomad tax havens. These havens cater specifically to the needs of digital nomads, offering favorable tax regimes that allow them to optimize their earnings. By understanding the tax benefits and considerations for digital nomads, bank regulators can ensure the smooth operation of these tax havens and attract a thriving community of digital nomads.

One key consideration for digital nomads is the concept of tax residency. Unlike traditional workers, digital nomads have the flexibility to choose their tax residency based on their lifestyle and personal preferences. This presents an opportunity for bank regulators to develop tax policies that attract digital nomads, encouraging them to establish residency in their jurisdictions.

Additionally, bank regulators should be aware of the tax benefits associated with digital nomadism. Digital nomads often have access to a wide range of deductions and exemptions specific to their unique lifestyle. These may include deductions for travel expenses, home office setups, and even technology equipment. By understanding these benefits, bank regulators can ensure that digital nomads are aware of the incentives available to them.

Furthermore, bank regulators should consider the implications of cryptocurrencies for digital nomads. Cryptocurrency tax havens can provide digital nomads with additional opportunities to optimize their tax positions. By embracing the use of cryptocurrencies, bank regulators can attract a tech-savvy community of digital nomads while also staying at the forefront of the evolving financial landscape.

In conclusion, understanding the tax benefits and considerations for digital nomads is crucial for bank regulators overseeing offshore banking tax havens. By recognizing the unique needs of digital nomads and developing favorable tax policies, bank regulators can attract and retain this vibrant community. Furthermore, by embracing the use of cryptocurrencies and staying abreast of the latest trends, bank regulators can position themselves as leaders in the ever-evolving world of offshore banking tax havens.

Residence and Citizenship Options

In today's globalized world, individuals and businesses have a wide range of options when it comes to choosing a residence or obtaining citizenship. These options have become particularly attractive to those interested in offshore banking tax havens, digital nomad tax havens, retirement tax havens, cryptocurrency tax havens, asset protection tax havens, estate planning tax havens, high-net-worth individual tax havens, business tax havens, real estate investment tax havens, and privacy-focused tax havens.

Offshore banking tax havens offer individuals and businesses the opportunity to establish accounts in jurisdictions with favorable tax and regulatory environments. These jurisdictions often have low or zero tax rates on interest income, capital gains, and inheritance. Bank regulators must stay informed about the latest developments in these jurisdictions to effectively regulate offshore banking activities and ensure compliance with international standards.

Digital nomad tax havens have emerged as a popular option for remote workers and location-independent entrepreneurs. These jurisdictions offer tax incentives and flexible residency options for individuals who work online. Bank regulators need to understand the unique challenges and risks associated with digital nomad tax havens, such as money laundering and fraud, to effectively regulate banking activities in these jurisdictions.

Retirement tax havens have long been a popular choice for individuals seeking a low-tax and high-quality lifestyle during their golden years. Bank regulators should be familiar with the different retirement tax havens and their specific regulations to ensure that retirees' financial interests are protected.

Cryptocurrency tax havens have gained attention in recent years as digital currencies continue to grow in popularity. These jurisdictions offer favorable tax treatment for cryptocurrency investors and businesses, attracting a significant number of individuals and companies in this sector. Bank regulators must stay up-to-date with the evolving regulatory landscape surrounding cryptocurrencies to effectively regulate banking activities related to digital assets.

Asset protection tax havens provide individuals with the means to safeguard their wealth from potential lawsuits, creditors, or other financial risks. Bank regulators need to understand the legal and regulatory frameworks of these jurisdictions to ensure that appropriate safeguards are in place to protect the interests of both clients and the banking sector.

Estate planning tax havens offer individuals and families the opportunity to structure their wealth and assets in a tax-efficient manner, ensuring smooth succession and minimizing tax liabilities for future generations. Bank regulators must be well-versed in the estate planning laws and regulations of these jurisdictions to oversee banking activities related to estate planning effectively.

High-net-worth individual tax havens cater to individuals with substantial wealth and provide a range of services tailored to their needs. Bank regulators need to have a deep understanding of the specific risks and challenges associated with servicing high-net-worth individuals to ensure compliance with anti-money laundering and other regulatory requirements.

Business tax havens attract entrepreneurs and corporations with favorable tax regimes, business-friendly regulations, and access to international markets. Bank regulators must monitor banking activities in these jurisdictions to prevent money laundering, tax evasion, and other illicit financial activities.

Real estate investment tax havens offer attractive investment opportunities for individuals and businesses looking to diversify their portfolios and take advantage of favorable tax incentives. Bank regulators must be familiar with the real estate markets and regulations of these jurisdictions to effectively oversee banking activities related to real estate investments.

Privacy-focused tax havens provide individuals and businesses with a high level of financial privacy and confidentiality. Bank regulators must strike a balance between privacy rights and the need to prevent money laundering, terrorist financing, and other illicit activities in these jurisdictions.

Overall, understanding the various residence and citizenship options available in offshore banking tax havens is crucial for bank regulators. By staying informed about the specific risks, challenges, and regulatory frameworks associated with these niches, regulators can effectively oversee banking activities, ensure compliance with international standards, and protect the interests of clients and the banking sector as a whole.

Tax Deductions for Digital Nomads

In today's ever-evolving digital age, more and more individuals are embracing the lifestyle of digital nomads. These intrepid individuals have ditched the traditional office environment in favor of working remotely, often while traveling the world. As bank regulators in the realm of offshore banking, it is essential to understand the unique tax implications that digital nomads face.

Digital nomads are a distinct group of individuals who typically work as freelancers, remote employees, or online entrepreneurs. They have the freedom to choose their location and often take advantage of the tax benefits offered by various jurisdictions. This subchapter will explore the tax deductions available to digital nomads and the potential impact on offshore banking.

One significant advantage for digital nomads is the ability to deduct certain expenses related to their work. Common deductions include travel expenses, such as flights, accommodation, and meals, as long as they are directly related to business activities. Additionally, expenses for necessary equipment, such as laptops, smartphones, and internet subscriptions, can also be deducted.

Many tax havens offer attractive tax deductions for digital nomads. These jurisdictions recognize the value that digital nomads bring to their economies and understand the unique nature of their work. By offering tax incentives, such as reduced or zero income tax rates, these tax havens attract digital nomads and encourage them to establish offshore banking relationships within their jurisdictions.

Furthermore, digital nomads who engage in cryptocurrency activities can benefit from tax deductions specific to this emerging asset class. Some tax havens provide tax breaks for cryptocurrency transactions, making them even more attractive to digital nomads who are active in this space.

As bank regulators, it is crucial to understand the impact of these tax deductions on the offshore banking industry. The influx of digital nomads to tax havens can lead to increased demand for banking services and the growth of the local economy. However, it is equally important to ensure that these tax deductions are not being misused for illicit purposes, such as money laundering or tax evasion. Robust regulatory measures must be in place to protect the integrity of the offshore banking system.

In conclusion, tax deductions play a vital role in attracting digital nomads to tax havens. By offering favorable tax incentives, jurisdictions can benefit from the economic contributions of this unique group of individuals. However, it is imperative for bank regulators to strike a balance between promoting offshore banking growth and maintaining strict regulatory oversight to prevent misuse. Understanding the tax deductions available to digital nomads is essential for navigating the offshore banking landscape in the digital age.

Managing Taxes Across Multiple Jurisdictions

In today's globalized economy, managing taxes across multiple jurisdictions is a crucial aspect of offshore banking. As bank regulators, it is essential to understand the complexities and implications of taxation in various offshore banking tax havens. This subchapter explores the intricacies of navigating tax systems in different jurisdictions, catering to the diverse needs of digital nomads, retirees, cryptocurrency enthusiasts, high-net-worth individuals, businesses, real estate investors, and those seeking privacy and asset protection.

1. Understanding Tax Havens:

Tax havens provide attractive tax benefits such as low or zero tax rates, privacy, and asset protection. In this section, we delve into the characteristics of offshore banking tax havens and how they cater to different niches. We explore why digital nomads, retirees, cryptocurrency enthusiasts, and others may choose specific tax havens to optimize their tax liabilities.

2. Tax Planning for Different Niches:

This section focuses on tax planning strategies for specific niches. We provide insights into how digital nomads can structure their income and assets to minimize tax obligations. We discuss retirement tax havens and the tax implications of relocating to these jurisdictions. Additionally, we explore cryptocurrency tax havens and the tax considerations for individuals and businesses involved in the crypto space.

3. Asset Protection and Estate Planning:

For high-net-worth individuals, asset protection and estate planning are paramount. We highlight tax havens that offer robust legal frameworks for safeguarding assets and minimizing estate taxes. We discuss the importance of trusts, foundations, and other legal structures in estate planning and asset protection.

4. Business Tax Havens and Real Estate Investment:

Business tax havens offer attractive tax incentives for companies seeking to optimize their tax liabilities. We explore the benefits of setting up businesses in these jurisdictions and how to navigate the tax landscape. Additionally, we discuss real estate investment tax havens and the tax implications of investing in properties abroad.

5. Privacy-Focused Tax Havens:

Privacy is a significant concern for many individuals and businesses. We explore tax havens that prioritize privacy and discuss the measures taken to protect financial information and maintain confidentiality.

In conclusion, managing taxes across multiple jurisdictions is a critical aspect of offshore banking. As bank regulators, understanding the nuances of taxation in various tax havens is essential. This subchapter provides valuable insights into tax planning for digital nomads, retirees, cryptocurrency enthusiasts, high-net-worth individuals, businesses, real estate investors, and those seeking privacy and asset protection. By navigating the complexities of tax systems in different jurisdictions, bank regulators can ensure compliance, facilitate informed decision-making, and support the growth of offshore banking in a responsible and sustainable manner.

Chapter 4: Retirement Tax Havens

Overview of Retirement Tax Havens

Retirement tax havens have gained significant attention in recent years as individuals seek to maximize their savings and enjoy a comfortable retirement. These havens offer attractive tax benefits and a favorable regulatory environment for retirees to manage their finances effectively. In this subchapter, we will explore the key features and benefits of retirement tax havens, specifically tailored for bank regulators who play a crucial role in overseeing offshore banking activities.

Retirement tax havens provide retirees with a range of financial advantages. One of the primary benefits is the low or zero tax rates on retirement income, including pensions, annuities, and investment gains. This allows retirees to keep a larger portion of their earnings, enhancing their financial security during their golden years. Additionally, these havens often offer exemptions or reduced rates on capital gains taxes, further incentivizing retirees to invest and grow their wealth.

Another advantage of retirement tax havens is the flexibility they offer in estate planning. Many retirees wish to pass on their wealth to their loved ones, and these havens provide favorable conditions for wealth transfer, including minimal inheritance taxes and streamlined probate processes. As bank regulators, understanding the intricacies of estate planning tax havens is crucial to ensure compliance and prevent any potential misuse.

Furthermore, retirement tax havens often boast a robust financial infrastructure with a range of investment opportunities. These havens attract high-net-worth individuals and businesses, leading to a vibrant investment landscape that retirees can tap into. Regulators must monitor these investment activities to ensure they are conducted in a transparent and lawful manner, safeguarding the interests of retirees.

Privacy-focused tax havens are also relevant to retirement tax havens, as retirees seek to protect their personal and financial information. Bank regulators must strike a balance between privacy and transparency to combat financial crimes while respecting the privacy rights of individuals.

In conclusion, retirement tax havens offer retirees a unique opportunity to optimize their finances and enjoy a prosperous retirement. As bank regulators, understanding the nuances of these havens is essential to effectively oversee offshore banking activities and ensure compliance. By staying informed about retirement tax havens, regulators can effectively protect retirees' interests while upholding the integrity of the financial system.

Popular Retirement Tax Havens

Retirement is a time of relaxation, exploration, and enjoying the fruits of one's labor. For many individuals, this period marks the beginning of a well-deserved break from the corporate world. However, as bank regulators, it is important to understand the different avenues retirees may take when it comes to managing their finances and taxes. In this subchapter, we will dive into the world of popular retirement tax havens, exploring the benefits and considerations associated with each.

Retirees often seek tax havens that offer financial advantages, a high quality of life, and favorable tax policies. One such popular destination is Panama. This Central American country boasts a low cost of living, warm climate, and excellent healthcare facilities. Panama's "Pensionado" program allows retirees to enjoy significant tax benefits, including tax exemptions on foreign-earned income, import tax exemptions, and reductions on property taxes.

Another attractive option is Portugal, which has gained prominence among retirees due to its Non-Habitual Resident (NHR) regime. Under this program, individuals who become tax residents of Portugal can benefit from a flat tax rate of 10% for certain types of foreign income, including pensions. Portugal also offers a relaxed lifestyle, beautiful landscapes, and a rich cultural heritage.

For those seeking a tropical paradise, the Caribbean island of Barbados is a popular choice. With its favorable tax regime for retirees, including a low personal income tax rate and exemptions on foreign income, retirees can enjoy a high standard of living in this idyllic location. Additionally, Barbados offers a stable political and economic environment, making it an attractive option for those looking to enjoy their golden years in the sun.

Other notable retirement tax havens include Belize, Costa Rica, and Malaysia, each offering unique advantages such as low cost of living, favorable tax policies, and welcoming environments for retirees.

As regulators, it is important to stay informed about these popular retirement tax havens. Understanding the benefits and considerations associated with each destination can help us ensure compliance and transparency in offshore banking activities. By familiarizing ourselves with the intricacies of retirement tax havens, we can better assist retirees in making informed decisions about their financial future.

In conclusion, popular retirement tax havens provide retirees with the opportunity to enjoy their golden years in a tax-efficient manner. From the lush landscapes of Portugal to the pristine beaches of Barbados, these destinations offer a range of benefits tailored to meet the needs and desires of retirees. By understanding the various retirement tax havens available, bank regulators can effectively navigate the offshore banking landscape and provide valuable guidance to individuals seeking to retire in these tax-friendly jurisdictions.

Panama

Panama is renowned for its status as a prominent offshore banking tax haven, making it a subject of interest for bank regulators worldwide. This subchapter aims to discuss the various aspects of Panama's offshore banking industry and its implications for different niches, including digital nomads, retirees, cryptocurrency enthusiasts, high-net-worth individuals, business owners, real estate investors, and those seeking privacy-focused tax havens.

Panama's appeal as an offshore banking tax haven stems from its favorable tax laws, robust financial infrastructure, and strict privacy regulations. The country offers a variety of services, including offshore bank accounts, wealth management, trust services, and company formation. Bank regulators need to understand the intricacies of these services to effectively oversee and regulate the activities within this sector.

For digital nomads, Panama presents a tax haven where they can manage their global income while benefiting from low tax rates and flexible residency options. Retirees, on the other hand, can take advantage of Panama's special retirement visa program, which offers enticing tax advantages and attractive retirement packages.

Cryptocurrency tax havens have gained prominence in recent years, and Panama has emerged as a favorable destination for crypto enthusiasts. Its cryptocurrency-friendly legislation and favorable tax treatment for crypto-related activities make it an attractive option for individuals and businesses operating in this space.

Panama also serves as an asset protection tax haven, offering a secure environment for safeguarding wealth and shielding assets from potential risks. Its strong legal framework and trust laws enable individuals to protect their assets from creditors, lawsuits, and other potential threats.

Estate planning tax havens play a crucial role in preserving generational wealth, and Panama's trust and foundation laws make it an ideal destination for such purposes. High-net-worth individuals can benefit from Panama's wealth management services, which include asset allocation, investment advisory, and succession planning.

Business tax havens attract entrepreneurs seeking favorable tax environments for their ventures. Panama's business-friendly policies, low corporate tax rates, and efficient company registration process make it an attractive destination for establishing offshore companies and conducting international business operations.

Real estate investment tax havens provide opportunities for investors to diversify their portfolios and enjoy tax advantages. Panama's stable economy, growing real estate market, and incentives for foreign investors make it an appealing destination for real estate investments.

Lastly, Panama caters to those seeking privacy-focused tax havens, as it maintains strict confidentiality laws that protect the privacy of individuals and businesses operating within its jurisdiction.

Overall, this subchapter aims to provide bank regulators with a comprehensive understanding of Panama's offshore banking industry and its implications for a wide range of niches. By examining these aspects, regulators can effectively assess and regulate offshore banking activities within this tax haven.

Belize

Belize: An Emerging Offshore Banking Haven

Belize, a small Central American country nestled between Mexico and Guatemala, has emerged as a promising destination for offshore banking. With its favorable tax regulations, flexible banking laws, and a robust financial sector, Belize offers an attractive environment for both individuals and businesses seeking to optimize their financial affairs.

For bank regulators, understanding the dynamics of offshore banking in Belize is crucial in ensuring the integrity and stability of the global financial system. This subchapter delves into the various aspects of Belize's offshore banking sector, shedding light on its potential benefits and challenges.

Offshore Banking Tax Haven:

Belize has established itself as a reputable offshore banking tax haven, attracting individuals and businesses seeking to reduce their tax liabilities legally. With a favorable tax regime, including no capital gains tax, estate tax, or inheritance tax, Belize offers an attractive environment for tax planning and wealth preservation.

Digital Nomad Tax Haven:

As the digital nomad lifestyle gains popularity, Belize has become a preferred destination for remote workers. Its low cost of living, beautiful landscapes, and tax advantages make it an ideal location for digital nomads looking to optimize their tax obligations while enjoying a high quality of life.

Retirement Tax Haven:

Belize offers a retiree-friendly environment with its Qualified Retirement Program (QRP). This initiative allows individuals aged 45 and above to qualify for tax exemptions on their foreign income and assets. The program also grants retirees the opportunity to import personal belongings duty-free, making Belize an attractive option for those seeking a peaceful and affordable retirement.

Cryptocurrency Tax Haven:

With its progressive stance on cryptocurrencies, Belize has positioned itself as a cryptocurrency tax haven. The country has implemented legislation to regulate and facilitate cryptocurrency activities, attracting investors and businesses operating in this digital asset space.

Asset Protection Tax Haven:

Belize's trust legislation provides a robust framework for asset protection. The country's International Business Companies (IBCs) and trusts offer individuals and businesses a secure and confidential way to protect their assets from potential legal claims or creditors.

Estate Planning Tax Haven:

Belize's trust laws also make it an ideal jurisdiction for estate planning. The country allows for the creation of dynastic trusts, enabling families to preserve and pass on their wealth for generations, while minimizing estate taxes and maintaining confidentiality.

High-Net-Worth Individual Tax Haven:

Belize provides an array of financial services tailored to high-net-worth individuals (HNWIs). From private banking and wealth management to trust services and family offices, Belize offers a comprehensive suite of solutions to meet the complex financial needs of HNWIs.

Business Tax Haven:

Belize's business-friendly environment, with its low corporate tax rates and simplified company registration process, attracts entrepreneurs and companies seeking a favorable tax regime and ease of doing business.

Real Estate Investment Tax Haven:

Belize's thriving real estate market, coupled with its tax advantages, makes it an attractive destination for real estate investors. The country offers opportunities for both residential and commercial property investments, with favorable tax treatment on rental income and capital gains.

Privacy-Focused Tax Haven:

Belize's strict confidentiality laws and robust banking secrecy provisions make it an ideal privacy-focused tax haven. The country ensures the highest level of privacy and confidentiality for individuals and businesses seeking to protect their financial information from prying eyes.

In conclusion, Belize offers a range of opportunities for individuals and businesses seeking to optimize their financial affairs in various niches of offshore banking. However, as bank regulators, it is essential to strike a balance between facilitating legitimate financial activities and preventing illicit financial practices in this evolving offshore banking landscape.

Mexico

Mexico has long been recognized as a popular offshore banking tax haven, attracting a diverse range of individuals and businesses seeking favorable tax advantages and asset protection. With its robust financial sector, stable economy, and strategic geographic location, Mexico offers an array of opportunities for bank regulators to explore and understand.

For those interested in digital nomad tax havens, Mexico presents an attractive option. Its affordable cost of living, reliable infrastructure, and vibrant expat communities make it an ideal destination for remote workers. Bank regulators can study the local banking regulations and incentives that attract digital nomads, helping them navigate the intricacies of offshore banking in this context.

Moreover, Mexico's retirement tax havens cater to the needs of individuals looking to enjoy their golden years in a financially advantageous manner. Bank regulators can delve into the retirement-specific financial products and services offered by Mexican banks, ensuring compliance and providing guidance to retirees seeking to make the most of their assets.

In recent years, Mexico has also emerged as a cryptocurrency tax haven. The country's progressive stance on digital currencies and blockchain technology has attracted crypto enthusiasts and investors. Bank regulators can examine the regulatory framework surrounding cryptocurrency transactions and explore how offshore banking can accommodate this growing sector.

Additionally, Mexico offers excellent opportunities for asset protection and estate planning tax havens. With a well-established legal system and favorable trust laws, individuals and families can safeguard their assets and plan for future generations. Bank regulators can study the intricacies of these mechanisms to effectively regulate and supervise offshore banking activities in this context.

High-net-worth individuals seeking tax advantages can find solace in Mexico's business tax havens. The country's favorable corporate tax rates and incentives make it an enticing destination for entrepreneurs and investors alike. Bank regulators can provide guidance on compliance requirements and ensure transparency within the offshore banking sector.

Mexico also offers attractive real estate investment tax havens, with its booming property market and ever-increasing demand for vacation rentals. Bank regulators can explore the regulations surrounding real estate investments and work towards creating a transparent and sustainable environment for offshore banking in this niche.

Lastly, Mexico serves as a privacy-focused tax haven, attracting individuals and businesses seeking to protect their financial information. Bank regulators can examine the legal framework surrounding privacy and data protection, ensuring that offshore banking activities maintain a balance between privacy and regulatory requirements.

In conclusion, Mexico offers a plethora of opportunities for bank regulators to navigate the complexities of offshore banking in various niches. By understanding the specific needs and demands of offshore banking tax havens, digital nomads, retirees, cryptocurrency enthusiasts, high-net-worth individuals, businesses, real estate investors, and privacy-focused individuals, bank regulators can effectively regulate and supervise the offshore banking sector in Mexico.

Portugal

Portugal: A Rising Star in Offshore Banking and Tax Havens

Portugal, a country known for its rich history, stunning landscapes, and vibrant culture, has emerged as a rising star in the world of offshore banking and tax havens. With its strategic location, stable economy, and favorable tax laws, Portugal offers numerous advantages for individuals and businesses seeking to optimize their financial affairs.

One of the key attractions of Portugal as an offshore banking destination is its non-habitual residency (NHR) regime. This regime allows individuals to benefit from significant tax advantages for a period of ten years. Under the NHR, foreign-source income and certain types of capital gains are exempt from taxation, making it an ideal choice for digital nomads, retirees, and high-net-worth individuals looking to minimize their tax burden.

Furthermore, Portugal has positioned itself as a hub for cryptocurrency enthusiasts and investors. The country has implemented progressive regulations to attract blockchain startups and has taken steps to encourage the use of cryptocurrencies in everyday transactions. This favorable environment, combined with the absence of capital gains tax on cryptocurrencies, makes Portugal an attractive option for those involved in the cryptocurrency industry.

In addition to its tax advantages, Portugal offers excellent asset protection opportunities. The country's legal framework provides strong protection of assets, making it an ideal choice for individuals seeking to safeguard their wealth. Moreover, Portugal's estate planning laws are designed to facilitate the seamless transfer of assets to future generations, ensuring a smooth and efficient process for estate planning.

For businesses, Portugal offers a business-friendly environment with attractive tax incentives. The country's corporate tax rate is one of the lowest in Europe, and it provides various tax breaks and incentives for businesses operating in specific sectors. Moreover, Portugal's membership in the European Union provides businesses with access to a large market and numerous trade opportunities.

Real estate investment in Portugal is also highly advantageous. The country's Golden Visa program offers residency to non-EU citizens who invest in Portuguese real estate, providing a gateway to Europe for investors. Additionally, Portugal's real estate market has experienced significant growth in recent years, making it an attractive investment opportunity for individuals and businesses alike.

Lastly, for those seeking privacy-focused tax havens, Portugal offers a high level of confidentiality. The country has implemented strict data protection laws and maintains a robust banking secrecy tradition, ensuring the privacy and confidentiality of individuals' financial information.

In conclusion, Portugal has emerged as an attractive offshore banking and tax haven destination for a wide range of individuals and businesses. With its favorable tax laws, asset protection opportunities, business incentives, and privacy-focused environment, Portugal provides an ideal setting for those looking to optimize their financial affairs. As bank regulators, it is crucial to stay informed about the advantages and risks associated with offshore banking in Portugal to effectively regulate this growing sector.

Malaysia

Malaysia: An Emerging Offshore Banking Destination

In recent years, Malaysia has emerged as one of the most promising offshore banking destinations globally. With its robust financial infrastructure, favorable tax regulations, and strategic geographic location, Malaysia offers numerous opportunities for both individuals and businesses seeking to enhance their financial portfolios.

For bank regulators, understanding the unique characteristics and benefits of Malaysia as an offshore banking tax haven is crucial. This subchapter aims to provide an overview of Malaysia's key features and advantages, catering specifically to the needs and interests of bank regulators and the various niches in the offshore banking industry.

One of the primary attractions of Malaysia is its digital nomad tax haven status. With a favorable tax regime for foreign-sourced income, digital nomads can benefit from Malaysia's territorial taxation system, which ensures that only income generated within the country is taxable. This incentive has attracted a growing number of location-independent professionals to choose Malaysia as their base of operations, contributing to the country's vibrant and diverse digital nomad community.

Moreover, Malaysia offers attractive retirement tax havens for individuals seeking a secure and affordable retirement destination. The Malaysia My Second Home (MM2H) program provides a range of incentives, including tax exemptions on offshore income and the ability to remit funds overseas. These benefits, coupled with Malaysia's high standard of living, modern healthcare facilities, and cultural diversity, make it an ideal retirement haven for individuals seeking a comfortable and fulfilling lifestyle.

Additionally, Malaysia has positioned itself as a cryptocurrency tax haven, fostering an environment conducive to blockchain technology and digital currencies. The government's proactive approach to regulating cryptocurrencies and blockchain-based businesses has attracted numerous global players to establish their operations in Malaysia. Bank regulators must stay abreast of the evolving regulatory landscape in this niche, ensuring that the sector operates safely and efficiently.

Furthermore, Malaysia is renowned for its robust asset protection and estate planning tax havens. The country offers a range of trust structures and legal frameworks that provide individuals and businesses with secure mechanisms to protect and manage their assets. Bank regulators must ensure that these structures adhere to international best practices and maintain transparency and accountability.

In conclusion, Malaysia presents a wealth of opportunities for bank regulators and the diverse niches within the offshore banking industry. Its favorable tax regulations, digital nomad and retirement tax havens, cryptocurrency-friendly environment, asset protection and estate planning structures, and other incentives make it an attractive destination for individuals and businesses alike. By understanding and navigating the unique aspects of Malaysia's offshore banking landscape, bank regulators can effectively regulate and oversee the industry, ensuring its stability and growth while safeguarding the interests of all stakeholders.

Retirement Planning Considerations in Tax Havens

Retirement planning is a critical aspect of financial management, and for those considering offshore banking in tax havens, it becomes even more important to understand the implications and considerations specific to this niche. In this subchapter, we delve into various factors that bank regulators should be aware of when it comes to retirement planning in tax havens.

Tax havens, known for their attractive tax benefits and investment opportunities, have become increasingly popular among a diverse range of individuals and entities. This includes digital nomads, high-net-worth individuals, cryptocurrency enthusiasts, and those seeking asset protection, estate planning, business opportunities, real estate investments, and privacy. However, the specific considerations for retirement planning in these jurisdictions vary depending on the niche.

For digital nomads, retirement planning may involve ensuring a steady income stream, managing tax obligations both in the current jurisdiction and the future tax haven, and exploring investment options that align with their lifestyle. Cryptocurrency tax havens, on the other hand, pose unique challenges related to the volatility of digital assets and the need for secure storage and access to funds as individuals transition into retirement.

Retirement tax havens, often known for their favorable retirement schemes and pension plans, offer various benefits for retirees, such as tax breaks, healthcare options, and a high standard of living. Bank regulators need to be knowledgeable about the specific retirement schemes available in these jurisdictions, ensuring compliance and transparency.

Asset protection tax havens can provide retirees with a secure environment to safeguard their wealth from potential risks. Estate planning tax havens may offer favorable inheritance laws and tax benefits, allowing retirees to pass on their wealth efficiently to future generations.

High-net-worth individuals, business owners, and real estate investors may have complex retirement planning needs. Bank regulators must be well-versed in the legal and financial intricacies of these tax havens to ensure compliance and effective supervision.

Privacy-focused tax havens play a significant role for retirees who value their financial privacy. Bank regulators should understand the legal frameworks surrounding privacy rights and data protection in these jurisdictions.

In summary, retirement planning considerations in tax havens vary across different niches. Bank regulators must possess a comprehensive understanding of these nuances to effectively regulate and supervise offshore banking activities. By being well-informed, they can ensure compliance, transparency, and protect the interests of retirees in tax havens.

Pension and Social Security Benefits

In the world of offshore banking, one important aspect that bank regulators need to understand is the handling of pension and social security benefits. This subchapter aims to provide an overview of the considerations and challenges involved in managing these benefits in various offshore tax haven niches, including offshore banking tax havens, digital nomad tax havens, retirement tax havens, cryptocurrency tax havens, asset protection tax havens, estate planning tax havens, high-net-worth individual tax havens, business tax havens, real estate investment tax havens, and privacy-focused tax havens.

Offshore banking tax havens offer individuals the opportunity to optimize their pension and social security benefits by taking advantage of favorable tax policies. Regulators need to ensure that these tax havens have robust mechanisms in place to prevent tax evasion and comply with international standards to maintain their reputation as legitimate offshore financial centers.

Digital nomad tax havens attract location-independent professionals who often have unique challenges in managing their pension and social security benefits due to their transient lifestyle. Regulators should encourage the development of digital infrastructure that allows seamless transfer and access to these benefits across borders while ensuring compliance with tax regulations.

Retirement tax havens cater to individuals seeking a peaceful and financially secure retirement. Bank regulators should focus on ensuring that these tax havens have strong consumer protection measures in place, guaranteeing the safety and accessibility of pension and social security funds for retirees.

Cryptocurrency tax havens are increasingly popular among investors in digital assets. Regulators need to address the complexities of managing pension and social security benefits in this niche, including the proper valuation of cryptocurrency holdings and ensuring compliance with anti-money laundering and know-your-customer regulations.

Asset protection tax havens provide individuals with a secure environment to safeguard their wealth, including pension and social security benefits. Regulators should ensure that these tax havens have robust legal frameworks to protect these assets from potential creditors or legal disputes.

Estate planning tax havens offer individuals opportunities to efficiently pass on their wealth, including pension and social security benefits, to future generations. Regulators should monitor the implementation of inheritance laws and ensure transparency in the management of these assets.

High-net-worth individual tax havens attract affluent individuals seeking to optimize their financial affairs, including pension and social security benefits. Regulators should ensure that these tax havens have comprehensive reporting mechanisms to prevent money laundering and tax evasion by these high-net-worth individuals.

Business tax havens provide favorable tax environments for companies, including those managing pension and social security funds for their employees. Regulators should focus on ensuring that these tax havens have stringent governance and compliance requirements to protect the interests of employees and retirees.

Real estate investment tax havens offer opportunities for individuals to invest their pension and social security funds in lucrative real estate projects. Regulators should ensure that these tax havens have transparent property markets and enforce regulations to protect investors' interests.

Privacy-focused tax havens attract individuals who prioritize confidentiality in their financial affairs, including pension and social security benefits. Regulators should strike a balance between privacy and financial transparency to ensure compliance with international tax regulations and prevent illicit activities.

In conclusion, managing pension and social security benefits in offshore banking tax havens requires regulators to address unique challenges specific to each niche. By understanding and addressing these challenges, bank regulators can contribute to the development of a robust offshore banking industry that protects the interests of individuals and maintains the integrity of the global financial system.

Healthcare and Insurance Options

One of the key considerations for individuals and businesses when choosing an offshore banking jurisdiction is the availability and quality of healthcare and insurance options. Bank regulators need to be well-informed about the healthcare and insurance landscape in tax haven jurisdictions to ensure the well-being and protection of their clients.

Offshore banking tax havens, digital nomad tax havens, retirement tax havens, cryptocurrency tax havens, asset protection tax havens, estate planning tax havens, high-net-worth individual tax havens, business tax havens, real estate investment tax havens, and privacy-focused tax havens all attract a diverse range of clients from various walks of life. Therefore, understanding the healthcare and insurance options available in these jurisdictions is crucial to meet the needs and expectations of these individuals and businesses.

When it comes to healthcare, tax havens often offer a range of options, from public healthcare systems to private hospitals and clinics. Bank regulators should familiarize themselves with the quality, accessibility, and coverage provided by these systems. Additionally, understanding the eligibility criteria and the process for obtaining healthcare services in these tax havens is essential for effectively guiding clients.

Insurance options are another important aspect to consider. Offshore banking jurisdictions typically offer a wide array of insurance products, including health insurance, life insurance, property insurance, and liability insurance. Bank regulators should have an in-depth knowledge of the insurance market in these tax havens, including the types of coverage available, the reputation and financial stability of insurance providers, and any specific regulations governing insurance services.

Bank regulators should also be aware of any tax implications related to healthcare and insurance in offshore banking jurisdictions. Understanding the tax treatment of insurance premiums and healthcare expenses is crucial for providing accurate advice to clients.

In summary, healthcare and insurance options are vital considerations for individuals and businesses when choosing an offshore banking jurisdiction. Bank regulators must be well-versed in the healthcare and insurance landscape in tax haven jurisdictions to ensure the well-being and protection of their clients. By understanding the quality, accessibility, coverage, eligibility criteria, and tax implications of healthcare and insurance services, bank regulators can effectively guide their clients in making informed decisions and safeguarding their financial interests.

Taxation of Retirement Income

Retirement is a time for relaxation, exploration, and enjoying the fruits of one's labor. However, for individuals who have chosen to retire in offshore tax havens, understanding the taxation of retirement income becomes an essential aspect of financial planning. In this subchapter, we will explore the various considerations and strategies related to the taxation of retirement income in offshore banking tax havens, catering to the interests of bank regulators and the niches of offshore banking tax havens, digital nomad tax havens, retirement tax havens, cryptocurrency tax havens, asset protection tax havens, estate planning tax havens, high-net-worth individual tax havens, business tax havens, real estate investment tax havens, and privacy-focused tax havens.

When it comes to retirement income, offshore tax havens often offer attractive tax benefits. However, it is crucial for bank regulators and individuals alike to understand the specific rules and regulations governing the taxation of retirement income in each jurisdiction. This knowledge enables regulators to effectively oversee the banking activities and ensure compliance, while individuals can make informed decisions about their financial affairs.

One key aspect of retirement income taxation in offshore tax havens is the treatment of pensions and annuities. Some jurisdictions may offer tax exemptions or reduced tax rates on qualifying pension income, providing retirees with substantial savings. Understanding the eligibility criteria and the tax implications associated with these benefits is essential for bank regulators and individuals seeking to retire in these tax havens.

Additionally, the taxation of investment income, such as interest, dividends, and capital gains, requires careful consideration. Offshore tax havens often provide favorable tax treatment for such income, allowing retirees to maximize their returns and preserve their wealth. However, it is crucial to understand the reporting requirements and any limitations or restrictions imposed by the jurisdiction to ensure compliance.

Furthermore, with the rise of cryptocurrency and digital nomadism, the taxation of these emerging income sources has become a subject of interest for retirees in tax havens. Bank regulators must stay abreast of the evolving regulatory landscape surrounding cryptocurrencies and digital assets, ensuring that these income streams are appropriately taxed and accounted for.

In conclusion, the taxation of retirement income in offshore tax havens is a complex and multi-faceted topic. Bank regulators play a crucial role in overseeing the compliance of financial institutions and ensuring that individuals are aware of their tax obligations. By understanding the specific rules and regulations governing the taxation of retirement income in each jurisdiction, bank regulators can effectively navigate the intricacies of offshore banking tax havens and provide guidance to the various niches within this realm.

Chapter 5: Cryptocurrency Tax Havens

Introduction to Cryptocurrency Tax Havens

In recent years, the rise of cryptocurrencies has revolutionized the financial landscape, providing individuals and businesses with unprecedented opportunities for wealth accumulation and asset protection. As bank regulators, it is essential to understand the concept of cryptocurrency tax havens and their implications on offshore banking.

Cryptocurrency tax havens refer to those jurisdictions that offer favorable tax conditions and regulatory frameworks for individuals and businesses involved in cryptocurrency transactions. These havens provide a safe and secure environment for investors to leverage the benefits of cryptocurrencies while minimizing their tax liabilities.

For offshore banking tax havens, the emergence of cryptocurrency tax havens has created new possibilities. Traditional offshore banking centers are adapting to the changing financial landscape by incorporating cryptocurrencies into their banking services. These centers attract investors seeking offshore accounts and asset protection strategies specifically tailored for cryptocurrencies.

Digital nomad tax havens have also embraced cryptocurrencies, allowing individuals with location-independent lifestyles to manage their finances efficiently. These havens enable digital nomads to receive payments in cryptocurrencies, reducing the complexities associated with international banking and taxation.

Retirement tax havens have recognized the potential of cryptocurrencies to enhance retirement planning. By providing tax incentives and favorable regulations, these havens enable retirees to invest in cryptocurrencies and diversify their retirement portfolios.

Cryptocurrency tax havens have also become attractive to high-net-worth individuals seeking asset protection strategies. These havens offer secure storage options for cryptocurrencies, protecting them from potential risks such as theft or seizure.

Furthermore, estate planning tax havens have incorporated cryptocurrencies into their legal frameworks, allowing individuals to include digital assets in their estate plans. This ensures a smooth transfer of wealth to future generations.

Business tax havens have recognized the potential of cryptocurrencies to facilitate international trade and investment. By offering business-friendly regulations and tax incentives, these havens attract entrepreneurs and companies involved in the cryptocurrency ecosystem.

Real estate investment tax havens have also embraced cryptocurrencies, offering opportunities for investors to purchase properties using digital currencies. These havens provide a seamless transaction process and attractive investment returns.

Lastly, privacy-focused tax havens leverage the anonymity and security features of cryptocurrencies to protect individuals' financial privacy. These havens offer individuals a safe haven to conduct confidential financial transactions without the fear of intrusive surveillance.

In conclusion, the emergence of cryptocurrency tax havens has brought about significant changes in the offshore banking industry. As bank regulators, it is crucial to understand the intricacies of these havens to effectively regulate and monitor the activities within this evolving sector. By grasping the unique opportunities and challenges presented by cryptocurrency tax havens, regulators can ensure a secure and transparent financial environment for individuals and businesses.

Prominent Cryptocurrency Tax Havens

In recent years, the rapid rise of cryptocurrencies has given birth to a new breed of tax havens that cater specifically to the needs of digital nomads, high-net-worth individuals, and businesses involved in the cryptocurrency space. These jurisdictions, commonly known as cryptocurrency tax havens, offer a favorable regulatory environment and attractive tax incentives to attract and retain cryptocurrency investors and businesses.

One such prominent cryptocurrency tax haven is Switzerland. With its favorable legislation and progressive approach to cryptocurrencies, Switzerland has become a magnet for blockchain startups and individuals seeking a tax-friendly environment. The Swiss government has implemented clear regulations that provide legal certainty for cryptocurrency businesses, ensuring a safe and stable ecosystem for innovation and investment. Additionally, Switzerland's low corporate tax rates and its reputation for financial stability make it an ideal choice for high-net-worth individuals and businesses looking to optimize their tax liabilities.

Another notable cryptocurrency tax haven is Singapore. Known for its business-friendly environment, Singapore has embraced cryptocurrencies and blockchain technology with open arms. The city-state has implemented a comprehensive regulatory framework that promotes innovation while safeguarding against money laundering and terrorist financing risks. Singapore's attractive tax regime, which includes exemptions for certain types of cryptocurrency transactions, has positioned it as a preferred destination for businesses and individuals in the cryptocurrency industry.

In addition to Switzerland and Singapore, other jurisdictions that have emerged as prominent cryptocurrency tax havens include Malta, Gibraltar, and the Cayman Islands. These jurisdictions have recognized the potential of cryptocurrencies and have taken proactive steps to attract cryptocurrency businesses and investors. With their favorable tax regimes, regulatory frameworks, and infrastructure for cryptocurrency transactions, these jurisdictions have positioned themselves as leaders in the crypto space.

However, it is important for bank regulators to closely monitor the activities in these cryptocurrency tax havens. While they offer attractive tax incentives, there is a risk of potential abuse and money laundering. Therefore, bank regulators must strike a balance between fostering innovation and ensuring compliance with anti-money laundering and counter-terrorism financing regulations.

In conclusion, prominent cryptocurrency tax havens have emerged as attractive destinations for individuals and businesses involved in the cryptocurrency industry. By providing a favorable regulatory environment, attractive tax incentives, and a stable ecosystem for innovation, these jurisdictions have positioned themselves as leaders in the crypto space. However, bank regulators must exercise caution and vigilance to prevent potential abuses and ensure compliance with global regulations.

Malta

Malta: The Allure of Offshore Banking and Tax Havens

Introduction:

In recent years, Malta has emerged as one of the most prominent offshore banking tax havens, attracting a diverse range of individuals and businesses seeking to optimize their financial affairs. This subchapter explores the unique features and advantages that make Malta an attractive destination for various niches, including digital nomads, high-net-worth individuals, retirees, and businesses. Additionally, we will delve into Malta's suitability as a tax haven for cryptocurrency enthusiasts, asset protection, estate planning, real estate investment, and privacy-focused individuals.

1. Offshore Banking Tax Haven:

Malta offers a favorable tax regime with various incentives for offshore banking activities. Its efficient regulatory framework ensures transparency, while the absence of capital gains and wealth taxes further adds to its appeal. Bank regulators should take note of Malta's robust banking system, which is known for its stability, security, and adherence to international standards.

2. Digital Nomad Tax Haven:

For digital nomads seeking a tax-friendly environment, Malta ticks all the boxes. Its Global Residence Programme allows eligible individuals to benefit from a flat tax rate of 15% on foreign income remitted to Malta, making it an attractive option for those with location-independent income streams.

3. Retirement Tax Haven:

Malta offers retirees a favorable tax environment through its Retirement Programme, which allows individuals to benefit from a reduced tax rate of 15% on foreign income remitted to Malta. Moreover, its pleasant climate, low cost of living, and high-quality healthcare system make it an ideal retirement destination.

4. Cryptocurrency Tax Haven:

Malta's proactive approach towards blockchain and cryptocurrencies has earned it the reputation of being a cryptocurrency tax haven. The country has developed a comprehensive regulatory framework that provides legal certainty for businesses operating in the crypto sphere.

5. Asset Protection Tax Haven:

Malta's robust legal framework and wealth management options make it an excellent choice for asset protection. Its trust legislation, foundations, and protected cell companies offer individuals and businesses an array of structures for safeguarding their assets.

6. Estate Planning Tax Haven:

With its favorable inheritance tax regime, Malta is an attractive jurisdiction for estate planning purposes. Individuals can establish trusts or structures that facilitate the transfer of wealth to future generations while minimizing tax liabilities.

7. High-Net-Worth Individual (HNWI) Tax Haven:

Malta's HNWI tax regime offers a residency-by-investment program, providing eligible individuals with the opportunity to enjoy attractive tax benefits and a high standard of living.

8. Business Tax Haven:

Malta's business-friendly environment, low corporate tax rate of 35%, extensive network of double tax treaties, and skilled workforce make it an ideal location for establishing international business structures.

9. Real Estate Investment Tax Haven:

Malta's booming real estate market, coupled with its tax advantages, makes it an appealing destination for real estate investors. The country offers various incentives, such as the Residence Programme, which facilitates property investment for non-EU individuals.

10. Privacy-Focused Tax Haven:

Malta's strong data protection laws, coupled with its commitment to privacy, make it an attractive destination for individuals seeking to protect their personal information and financial affairs.

Conclusion:

Malta's strategic location, stable economy, favorable tax regime, and robust regulatory framework make it a top choice for individuals and businesses seeking offshore banking and tax havens. Bank regulators should carefully monitor the evolving landscape of Malta's offshore sector to ensure compliance with international standards while preserving the benefits it offers to various niches.

Switzerland

Switzerland: The Epitome of Offshore Banking Excellence

Switzerland has long been hailed as the epitome of offshore banking excellence, attracting a diverse range of individuals and businesses seeking to capitalize on its favorable tax laws, robust financial infrastructure, and unrivaled privacy protections. For bank regulators navigating the complex world of offshore banking, understanding the intricacies of Switzerland's banking system is crucial.

Offshore Banking Tax Havens: Switzerland's Timeless Appeal

Switzerland's reputation as a premier offshore banking tax haven remains unparalleled. With its stable economy, political neutrality, and low tax rates, it has become a magnet for individuals and businesses seeking to minimize their tax liabilities. Bank regulators must be well-versed in the legal and regulatory framework that underpins Switzerland's offshore banking sector to effectively monitor and regulate its activities.

Digital Nomad Tax Havens: Switzerland's Attractive Residency Programs

Switzerland's attractive residency programs make it an appealing destination for digital nomads seeking favorable tax treatment. The country offers a range of permits and visas designed to accommodate individuals who work remotely or operate location-independent businesses. Bank regulators must stay abreast of the evolving needs and requirements of digital nomads to ensure compliance with applicable regulations.

Retirement Tax Havens: Switzerland's Secure and Stable Environment

Switzerland's secure and stable environment, coupled with its favorable tax regime, makes it an ideal retirement tax haven. Bank regulators must understand the specific needs and challenges faced by retirees and ensure that the banking system provides the necessary safeguards and support to facilitate a comfortable retirement for individuals choosing Switzerland as their retirement destination.

Cryptocurrency Tax Havens: Switzerland's Progressive Approach

Switzerland's progressive approach to cryptocurrency regulation has positioned it as a leading destination for individuals and businesses operating in the crypto space. With its Crypto Valley in Zug and favorable tax treatment for cryptocurrency transactions, Switzerland attracts crypto enthusiasts from around the globe. Bank regulators must adapt to the unique regulatory challenges posed by cryptocurrencies and ensure that the banking system remains at the forefront of this rapidly evolving industry.

Asset Protection Tax Havens: Switzerland's Trusts and Foundations

Switzerland's robust legal framework for asset protection, including trusts and foundations, has made it a sought-after destination for individuals and businesses seeking to safeguard their wealth. Bank regulators must be well-versed in the intricacies of these structures to effectively regulate and monitor their use, preventing abuse and ensuring the integrity of the banking system.

Estate Planning Tax Havens: Switzerland's Wealth Management Expertise

Switzerland's long-standing reputation as a global wealth management hub makes it an attractive destination for estate planning purposes. Its sophisticated financial sector, coupled with its favorable tax laws, provides individuals with the necessary tools to effectively manage and distribute their wealth. Bank regulators must ensure that the banking system supports estate planning activities while maintaining transparency and compliance with relevant regulations.

High-Net-Worth Individual Tax Havens: Switzerland's Exclusive Private Banking Services

Switzerland's private banking services cater to the unique needs of high-net-worth individuals, providing personalized financial solutions and exceptional client service. Bank regulators must closely monitor these services to ensure that they adhere to strict regulatory standards, mitigating the risk of money laundering or other illicit activities.

Business Tax Havens: Switzerland's Business-Friendly Environment

Switzerland's business-friendly environment, coupled with its low corporate tax rates, has made it an attractive destination for companies looking to establish a presence in a tax-advantaged jurisdiction. Bank regulators must understand the specific needs and challenges faced by businesses operating in Switzerland and ensure that the banking system provides the necessary support and infrastructure to facilitate their operations.

Real Estate Investment Tax Havens: Switzerland's Stable Property Market

Switzerland's stable property market and favorable tax treatment for real estate investments make it an attractive destination for investors seeking to diversify their portfolios. Bank regulators must monitor real estate transactions to prevent money laundering and ensure compliance with anti-money laundering regulations.

Privacy-Focused Tax Havens: Switzerland's Commitment to Banking Secrecy

Switzerland's long-standing commitment to banking secrecy has made it a preferred destination for individuals and businesses seeking a high level of privacy and confidentiality. However, recent international initiatives aimed at combating tax evasion and money laundering have prompted Switzerland to adopt more transparent practices. Bank regulators must strike a delicate balance between privacy and transparency, ensuring that the banking system maintains its integrity while complying with international standards.

In conclusion, Switzerland's offshore banking sector offers a wide range of opportunities and challenges for bank regulators. Understanding the intricacies of Switzerland's banking system, its tax laws, and its commitment to privacy is essential for regulators to effectively navigate the complex world of offshore banking and ensure the integrity of the banking system.

Gibraltar

Gibraltar – A Leading Offshore Banking Tax Haven

Introduction:

In this subchapter, we will explore Gibraltar, a renowned offshore banking tax haven that offers a multitude of benefits to individuals and businesses alike. As bank regulators, understanding the dynamics of Gibraltar's offshore banking system is crucial to effectively oversee and regulate the operations in this tax haven, catering to various niches such as digital nomads, retirees, cryptocurrency enthusiasts, high-net-worth individuals, and more.

Overview of Gibraltar:

Situated at the southern tip of the Iberian Peninsula, Gibraltar is a British Overseas Territory known for its robust financial services sector. With a stable political environment, strong regulatory framework, and a well-developed infrastructure, Gibraltar has emerged as a preferred destination for offshore banking activities.

Tax Advantages:

Gibraltar offers attractive tax advantages, making it an ideal tax haven for various niches. Individuals and businesses can benefit from low corporate tax rates, zero capital gains tax, and no wealth tax. Moreover, Gibraltar has implemented a territorial tax system, ensuring that only locally sourced income is taxed, while foreign income remains tax-free.

Digital Nomad-Friendly:

Gibraltar has become increasingly popular among digital nomads due to its favorable tax policies and high-quality lifestyle. With a low personal income tax rate capped at 29%, digital nomads can enjoy the benefits of a tax-efficient environment while enjoying the vibrant culture, beautiful landscapes, and favorable climate that Gibraltar has to offer.

Cryptocurrency Haven:

As the digital currency revolution continues to gain momentum, Gibraltar has positioned itself as a leading jurisdiction for cryptocurrency-related activities. The territory has implemented a comprehensive regulatory framework for blockchain and cryptocurrency businesses, providing a secure and transparent environment for investors and entrepreneurs alike.

Asset Protection and Estate Planning:

Gibraltar offers robust asset protection and estate planning opportunities, making it an attractive tax haven for individuals looking to safeguard their wealth. With its strong legal system, trust legislation, and confidentiality provisions, Gibraltar enables individuals to protect their assets, optimize their estate planning, and ensure their financial privacy.

Privacy-Focused and Business-Friendly:

Gibraltar's offshore banking system provides a high level of financial privacy, attracting individuals and businesses seeking discretion. The territory offers a business-friendly environment with streamlined company formation procedures, minimal reporting requirements, and access to a skilled workforce, making it an ideal destination for entrepreneurs and investors.

Conclusion:

Gibraltar stands out as an exceptional offshore banking tax haven, catering to a wide range of niches such as digital nomads, retirees, cryptocurrency enthusiasts, high-net-worth individuals, and more. Its advantageous tax policies, robust regulatory framework, and attractive lifestyle make it a preferred choice for individuals and businesses looking to optimize their financial strategies. As bank regulators, understanding the intricacies of Gibraltar's offshore banking system is crucial to ensuring compliance and effective supervision in this tax haven.

Bermuda

Bermuda: A Premier Offshore Banking Tax Haven

As a bank regulator, it is essential to have a comprehensive understanding of offshore banking tax havens to effectively oversee the financial industry. Among the plethora of tax havens worldwide, Bermuda stands out as a premier destination for individuals and businesses seeking to optimize their financial affairs.

Located in the Atlantic Ocean, Bermuda has long been recognized for its favorable tax environment, making it an attractive choice for high-net-worth individuals, digital nomads, retirees, and businesses alike. This subchapter will delve into the key aspects of Bermuda's offshore banking landscape and shed light on its relevance to various niches within the tax haven industry.

For high-net-worth individuals seeking to protect and grow their assets, Bermuda offers a range of sophisticated wealth management services. Its financial institutions are renowned for their expertise in estate planning, asset protection, and privacy-focused solutions. Moreover, Bermuda's robust legal framework ensures the security and confidentiality of client information, instilling confidence in those who prioritize privacy.

Businesses also benefit from Bermuda's favorable tax regime, which includes no corporate income tax, capital gains tax, or withholding tax on dividends. This advantageous environment attracts companies from diverse sectors, such as real estate investment, international trade, and financial services. In addition, Bermuda's proximity to major international markets and its well-developed infrastructure make it an ideal hub for global business operations.

Digital nomads, a growing segment of the workforce, can take advantage of Bermuda's innovative policies. The jurisdiction recently introduced a "Work from Bermuda" program, allowing qualified individuals to reside and work remotely from the island for up to a year. This initiative combines the allure of living in a tropical paradise with the benefits of an offshore tax haven, creating an appealing option for professionals seeking a flexible lifestyle.

Furthermore, Bermuda has embraced the rise of cryptocurrencies, positioning itself as a cryptocurrency tax haven. The jurisdiction has implemented a progressive regulatory framework that fosters innovation while ensuring compliance with anti-money laundering and know-your-customer requirements. This approach has attracted blockchain-based businesses and cryptocurrency investors, solidifying Bermuda's position as a forward-thinking financial center.

In summary, Bermuda offers a comprehensive suite of advantages for those seeking offshore banking solutions. From its favorable tax environment to its commitment to privacy and innovation, the jurisdiction caters to a wide range of niches within the tax haven industry. As bank regulators, understanding the dynamics of Bermuda's offshore banking sector is crucial for effectively supervising financial institutions operating within this jurisdiction.

Singapore

Singapore: A Global Hub for Offshore Banking and Financial Services

Introduction:

Singapore, a prominent financial center in Asia, has emerged as one of the leading offshore banking tax havens. With its robust legal framework, political stability, and efficient financial infrastructure, Singapore offers a wide range of benefits for individuals and businesses seeking to optimize their financial strategies. This subchapter explores Singapore's position as a preferred destination for offshore banking and its relevance to various niches, including digital nomads, retirees, cryptocurrency enthusiasts, high-net-worth individuals, businesses, real estate investors, and those focused on privacy and asset protection.

1. Offshore Banking Tax Haven:

Singapore stands out as a premier offshore banking tax haven, offering numerous tax incentives and a low tax rate for foreign-sourced income. Bank regulators can explore Singapore's comprehensive network of double tax treaties, which facilitate cross-border investments, enhance tax efficiency, and reduce withholding taxes. Moreover, Singapore's well-regulated financial sector ensures transparency and compliance with international standards, making it an attractive choice for bank regulators overseeing offshore banking activities.

2. Digital Nomad Tax Haven:

With the rise of digital nomads, Singapore has emerged as an ideal destination for individuals seeking a tax-friendly environment. Its favorable tax structure, absence of capital gains tax, and territorial tax system make Singapore an attractive option for remote workers and freelancers. Bank regulators can appreciate Singapore's innovation-driven economy, which fosters digital entrepreneurship and provides a conducive environment for digital nomads to thrive.

3. Retirement Tax Haven:

Singapore's stable economy, high standard of living, and excellent healthcare infrastructure make it an appealing retirement destination. Bank regulators can explore Singapore's retirement schemes, such as the Central Provident Fund (CPF), which offers comprehensive retirement benefits and ensures financial security during the golden years. Additionally, Singapore's tax-efficient policies and strong asset protection laws make it an attractive choice for retirees seeking to preserve and grow their wealth.

4. Cryptocurrency Tax Haven:

As the global interest in cryptocurrencies grows, Singapore has positioned itself as a cryptocurrency tax haven. Its progressive approach towards digital currencies, friendly regulatory environment, and strong investor protection measures have attracted numerous cryptocurrency exchanges and blockchain companies. Bank regulators can appreciate Singapore's efforts to promote innovation in the fintech sector while ensuring compliance with anti-money laundering and counter-terrorism financing regulations.

Conclusion:

For bank regulators overseeing offshore banking activities, Singapore offers a compelling proposition. Its reputation as a reputable offshore banking tax haven is bolstered by its strong legal framework, political stability, and efficient financial infrastructure. Whether it's catering to digital nomads, retirees, cryptocurrency enthusiasts, high-net-worth individuals, businesses, real estate investors, or those focused on privacy and asset protection, Singapore presents a wealth of opportunities. By understanding Singapore's unique advantages and regulatory landscape, bank regulators can navigate the complexities of offshore banking and foster a thriving financial ecosystem.

Regulatory Frameworks for Cryptocurrencies in Tax Havens

Cryptocurrencies have gained significant popularity and adoption in recent years, presenting new challenges and opportunities for bank regulators in tax havens. As the use of digital currencies continues to grow, it is crucial for regulators in offshore banking tax havens, digital nomad tax havens, retirement tax havens, cryptocurrency tax havens, asset protection tax havens, estate planning tax havens, high-net-worth individual tax havens, business tax havens, real estate investment tax havens, and privacy-focused tax havens to establish robust regulatory frameworks to ensure the integrity and stability of their financial systems.

One key aspect of regulating cryptocurrencies in tax havens is the identification and verification of cryptocurrency users. Implementing know-your-customer (KYC) and anti-money laundering (AML) procedures is essential to prevent illicit activities such as money laundering, terrorist financing, and fraud. Regulators should collaborate with cryptocurrency exchanges and service providers to ensure compliance with these regulations.

Furthermore, tax havens should develop clear guidelines on the taxation of cryptocurrencies. While some jurisdictions may choose to exempt cryptocurrencies from taxation, others may opt for a more comprehensive approach, considering digital currencies as assets subject to capital gains tax. Establishing transparent tax policies will provide clarity to individuals and businesses operating within the cryptocurrency ecosystem, facilitating compliance and reducing the risk of tax evasion.

Another critical aspect is the licensing and supervision of cryptocurrency exchanges and other service providers. Regulators should establish a licensing framework that ensures only reputable and competent entities can operate in the jurisdiction. Ongoing supervision and regular audits should be conducted to ensure compliance with regulations and to protect investors from potential risks associated with the volatility and security of cryptocurrencies.

In addition to licensing, regulators should also focus on consumer protection measures. Educating the public about the risks and benefits of cryptocurrencies is crucial for individuals to make informed investment decisions. Regulators should establish mechanisms for handling consumer complaints and disputes, ensuring that investors have recourse in case of fraudulent activities or mismanagement by cryptocurrency service providers.

Collaboration with international regulatory bodies and standard-setting organizations is also essential. The fast-paced nature of cryptocurrencies requires regulators to stay updated with global developments and best practices. Sharing information and experiences with other tax havens can help develop a harmonized approach to regulating cryptocurrencies while maintaining the unique advantages offered by each jurisdiction.

In conclusion, the rise of cryptocurrencies presents both opportunities and challenges for bank regulators in tax havens. By establishing robust regulatory frameworks that encompass KYC/AML procedures, clear tax policies, licensing and supervision requirements, consumer protection measures, and international collaboration, tax havens can ensure the integrity and stability of their financial systems while embracing the potential benefits of digital currencies for their respective niches.

Licensing and Registration Requirements

Introduction:

In today's globalized financial landscape, offshore banking tax havens have become increasingly popular among individuals and businesses seeking to optimize their financial strategies. However, as bank regulators, it is crucial to understand the licensing and registration requirements associated with offshore banking to ensure the integrity and stability of the financial system. This subchapter will delve into the key considerations and regulations surrounding licensing and registration for various niches within the offshore banking industry, including digital nomad tax havens, retirement tax havens, cryptocurrency tax havens, asset protection tax havens, estate planning tax havens, high-net-worth individual tax havens, business tax havens, real estate investment tax havens, and privacy-focused tax havens.

Licensing and Registration for Offshore Banking Tax Havens:

1. Digital Nomad Tax Havens:

Digital nomads, who rely on technology to work remotely, often seek tax havens that accommodate their transient lifestyle. Regulators should be aware of licensing requirements specific to these jurisdictions and ensure compliance with tax laws in both the home country and the tax haven.

2. Retirement Tax Havens:

Retirement tax havens cater to individuals looking to enjoy their golden years in a financially favorable environment. Bank regulators should understand the licensing and registration requirements in these jurisdictions to ensure the protection of retirees' assets and compliance with international tax regulations.

3. Cryptocurrency Tax Havens:

As cryptocurrencies gain widespread acceptance, certain jurisdictions have emerged as tax havens for digital asset investors. Bank regulators must stay abreast of the evolving regulations in this niche, including licensing requirements for cryptocurrency exchanges, wallets, and other related services.

4. Asset Protection Tax Havens:

Asset protection tax havens offer legal structures and favorable tax regimes to safeguard assets from potential creditors. Regulators should familiarize themselves with the licensing and registration requirements for trust companies, asset management firms, and other entities involved in asset protection strategies.

5. Estate Planning Tax Havens:

Individuals seeking to optimize their estate planning often turn to tax havens that provide favorable inheritance laws and tax benefits. Bank regulators need to understand the licensing requirements for estate planning services, including trust administration, wills, and estate management.

6. High-Net-Worth Individual Tax Havens:

High-net-worth individuals require sophisticated banking services tailored to their unique financial needs. Regulators must be well-versed in the licensing and registration requirements for private banking, wealth management, and family office services offered in these tax havens.

7. Business Tax Havens:

Business tax havens attract companies looking to optimize their tax liabilities and benefit from favorable regulatory environments. Bank regulators must have a comprehensive understanding of the licensing and registration requirements for offshore companies, international trading, and financial services aimed at businesses.

8. Real Estate Investment Tax Havens:

Tax havens that offer advantageous real estate investment opportunities require specific licensing and registration processes to ensure the legitimacy and transparency of transactions. Regulators should be knowledgeable about these requirements to prevent money laundering and illicit activities.

9. Privacy-Focused Tax Havens:

Privacy-focused tax havens attract individuals and businesses seeking to maintain confidentiality and protect their financial information.

Bank regulators should understand the licensing and registration requirements for entities providing financial services while ensuring compliance with anti-money laundering and know-your-customer regulations.

Conclusion:

Navigating the licensing and registration requirements within the offshore banking industry is paramount for bank regulators. Understanding the intricacies of various tax haven niches, such as digital nomad tax havens, retirement tax havens, cryptocurrency tax havens, and others, enables regulators to effectively oversee these jurisdictions, maintain financial stability, and ensure compliance with international standards.

AML and KYC Compliance

In the world of offshore banking, it is essential for bank regulators to understand and enforce Anti-Money Laundering (AML) and Know Your Customer (KYC) compliance regulations. These regulations play a crucial role in maintaining the integrity of the financial system and safeguarding against illicit activities such as money laundering, terrorist financing, and other financial crimes. This subchapter explores the importance of AML and KYC compliance in various niches of offshore banking tax havens, including digital nomad tax havens, retirement tax havens, cryptocurrency tax havens, asset protection tax havens, estate planning tax havens, high-net-worth individual tax havens, business tax havens, real estate investment tax havens, and privacy-focused tax havens.

Bank regulators must be well-versed in AML and KYC regulations to effectively oversee offshore banking activities in these tax havens. Digital nomad tax havens, for instance, attract individuals who work remotely while traveling the world. Such individuals may utilize offshore accounts for their banking needs, making it crucial for regulators to ensure that these accounts are not being misused for illicit purposes. Similarly, retirement tax havens cater to individuals looking to enjoy their golden years in a tax-friendly environment. Regulators must ensure that these jurisdictions are not being exploited for money laundering or other financial crimes.

With the rise of cryptocurrencies, cryptocurrency tax havens have emerged as popular destinations for investors seeking to benefit from the tax advantages offered by these jurisdictions. However, regulators must closely monitor these transactions to prevent the misuse of cryptocurrencies for money laundering or terrorist financing.

In addition to individual investors, high-net-worth individuals and businesses often seek out offshore banking for asset protection, estate planning, and tax optimization purposes. Regulators need to ensure that these activities comply with AML and KYC regulations to prevent abuse and maintain transparency in the financial system.

Furthermore, real estate investment tax havens and privacy-focused tax havens have their unique compliance challenges. Regulators must address potential risks associated with real estate investments, such as money laundering through property purchases. They also need to strike a balance between privacy and transparency to ensure that privacy-focused tax havens are not being exploited by criminals.

In conclusion, AML and KYC compliance are of utmost importance in various niches of offshore banking tax havens. Bank regulators must stay vigilant and enforce these regulations to maintain the integrity of the financial system and prevent financial crimes. By doing so, they can ensure that offshore banking tax havens continue to thrive as legitimate and transparent financial centers.

Tax Treatment of Cryptocurrency Transactions

Cryptocurrency has emerged as a new and exciting asset class, presenting unique challenges and opportunities in the realm of taxation. As bank regulators, it is crucial to understand the tax treatment of cryptocurrency transactions within the context of offshore banking. This subchapter aims to provide an overview of the key considerations and guidelines for tax regulators in navigating this rapidly evolving landscape.

Offshore Banking Tax Havens

Offshore banking tax havens have become popular destinations for cryptocurrency investors seeking favorable tax treatment. These jurisdictions often offer low or zero capital gains tax, no inheritance tax, and reduced reporting requirements. However, it is important for regulators to ensure that tax evasion and money laundering risks are adequately addressed.

Digital Nomad Tax Havens

Digital nomads, who frequently rely on cryptocurrencies for their cross-border transactions, may take advantage of tax havens that offer special incentives for remote workers. Regulators must consider the tax implications and ensure compliance with tax residency rules, as digital nomads often travel extensively and may have multiple sources of income.

Retirement Tax Havens

Retirement tax havens can be particularly attractive for cryptocurrency investors looking to secure their wealth for their golden years. Regulators should provide clear guidelines on the tax treatment of cryptocurrency assets held in retirement accounts, ensuring compliance with international tax reporting standards.

Cryptocurrency Tax Havens

Some jurisdictions have positioned themselves as cryptocurrency tax havens by offering favorable tax treatment specifically for digital assets. Regulators must stay vigilant to prevent abuse and ensure that these incentives are not exploited for illicit purposes.

Asset Protection Tax Havens

Cryptocurrencies provide opportunities for asset protection, allowing individuals to shield their assets from potential legal disputes or creditors. Regulators should carefully consider the tax implications and ensure that asset protection strategies involving cryptocurrencies are not used for illegal activities or tax evasion.

Estate Planning Tax Havens

Cryptocurrencies present unique challenges in estate planning, as they are often held in digital wallets and can be easily overlooked without proper documentation. Regulators should provide guidance on how to include cryptocurrencies in estate planning, ensuring that the transfer of digital assets is properly accounted for and taxed.

High-Net-Worth Individual Tax Havens

High-net-worth individuals who hold significant amounts of cryptocurrency may seek tax havens that offer preferential treatment for their wealth. Regulators must strike a balance between attracting these individuals and preventing tax evasion, ensuring that the tax treatment of cryptocurrencies is transparent and fair.

Business Tax Havens

Cryptocurrency transactions are increasingly being used in business operations. Regulators should provide clear guidelines on how businesses should account for and report cryptocurrency income, ensuring that tax obligations are met.

Real Estate Investment Tax Havens

Real estate investments financed through cryptocurrencies have gained popularity. Regulators should address the tax implications of such transactions, ensuring that the tax treatment is clear and aligned with international standards.

Privacy-Focused Tax Havens

Privacy-focused tax havens attract individuals seeking to maintain anonymity in their financial transactions. Regulators must carefully consider the privacy implications of cryptocurrencies while ensuring that tax evasion and money laundering risks are appropriately managed.

In conclusion, the tax treatment of cryptocurrency transactions in offshore banking tax havens requires careful consideration and regulation. Regulators must strike a balance between attracting investment and preventing tax evasion, ensuring that the tax treatment of cryptocurrencies is transparent, fair, and aligned with international standards.

Chapter 6: Asset Protection Tax Havens

Understanding Asset Protection Strategies

In the world of offshore banking, asset protection strategies play a vital role in safeguarding the interests of individuals and businesses. As bank regulators, it is crucial to have a comprehensive understanding of these strategies to effectively navigate the landscape of offshore banking tax havens, digital nomad tax havens, retirement tax havens, cryptocurrency tax havens, and various other niche areas such as estate planning tax havens, high-net-worth individual tax havens, business tax havens, real estate investment tax havens, and privacy-focused tax havens.

Asset protection strategies refer to legal techniques employed to shield assets from potential risks, such as creditors, litigation, or excessive taxation. These strategies aim to preserve wealth, maintain financial privacy, and provide peace of mind to individuals and businesses seeking to protect their assets in a globalized and interconnected world.

One key aspect of asset protection strategies involves the establishment of offshore trusts, foundations, or corporate entities in tax havens. Offshore banking tax havens, known for their favorable regulatory frameworks, provide individuals and businesses with attractive options to protect their assets. By placing assets in structures such as trusts or foundations, individuals can separate their personal and business assets, reducing the risk of them being seized or subject to excessive taxation.

Digital nomad tax havens, popular among individuals who work remotely while traveling, offer unique asset protection opportunities. These tax havens allow digital nomads to structure their income and assets in a tax-efficient manner, ensuring their hard-earned money is protected and their tax liability is minimized.

Retirement tax havens provide retirees with the opportunity to protect their savings and pension funds from potential risks. By leveraging the favorable tax and regulatory environment in these havens, retirees can ensure their financial security and enjoy the benefits of a well-structured retirement plan.

Cryptocurrency tax havens offer a safe haven for investors in the digital currency space. With the increasing popularity of cryptocurrencies, protecting these assets from hacking, theft, or regulatory uncertainties has become paramount. By utilizing the services of cryptocurrency tax havens, investors can secure their digital assets while capitalizing on the favorable tax treatment offered by these jurisdictions.

Asset protection tax havens, estate planning tax havens, high-net-worth individual tax havens, business tax havens, real estate investment tax havens, and privacy-focused tax havens all offer unique advantages for individuals and businesses seeking to protect their assets. Understanding the intricacies of each niche is essential for bank regulators as they ensure the integrity and stability of the offshore banking industry.

In conclusion, asset protection strategies are crucial for individuals and businesses operating in the offshore banking industry. By comprehending the nuances of various tax havens and their respective niches, bank regulators can effectively oversee and regulate this sector, fostering a secure and stable environment for the protection of assets in a globalized world.

Notable Asset Protection Tax Havens

In the world of offshore banking, there are several notable tax havens that specialize in providing asset protection solutions to individuals and businesses. These jurisdictions offer robust legal frameworks and favorable tax regimes, making them attractive options for those seeking to safeguard their wealth and assets.

One such tax haven is the Cayman Islands, renowned for its strong asset protection laws and flexible corporate structures. The jurisdiction provides a range of trusts and foundations that can be utilized for asset protection purposes. The Cayman Islands also offers a stable political and economic environment, making it a favored destination for high-net-worth individuals and corporations looking to preserve their wealth.

Another prominent asset protection tax haven is Switzerland. With its long history of financial stability and privacy, Switzerland has become synonymous with wealth preservation. The country's strong legal system and banking secrecy laws make it an ideal choice for individuals seeking to shield their assets from creditors and legal disputes. Swiss banks are renowned for their discretion and expertise in asset protection strategies, making them a trusted partner for many high-net-worth individuals.

For those in the digital nomad niche, Estonia offers an innovative and forward-thinking approach to asset protection. The country's e-Residency program allows individuals to establish a digital identity and access a range of online government services. This makes Estonia an attractive option for digital nomads looking to protect their assets while enjoying the freedom of location independence.

In the realm of cryptocurrency, the British Virgin Islands has emerged as a popular tax haven. With its favorable tax regime and flexible corporate structures, the jurisdiction has become a hub for cryptocurrency companies and investors. The British Virgin Islands offer a secure environment for holding digital assets and conducting business in the blockchain industry.

Other notable asset protection tax havens include Belize, Panama, and Nevis, which offer favorable asset protection laws and corporate structures. These jurisdictions provide a range of options for asset protection, including trusts and offshore companies.

It is important to note that while these tax havens offer attractive asset protection solutions, it is crucial for bank regulators to ensure compliance with international regulations and prevent illicit activities. Effective oversight and cooperation between regulators are essential to maintain the integrity and reputation of offshore banking jurisdictions.

In conclusion, asset protection tax havens provide individuals and businesses with a range of options to safeguard their wealth and assets. From traditional offshore banking destinations like Switzerland to innovative digital nomad tax havens like Estonia, these jurisdictions offer favorable legal frameworks and tax regimes for asset protection. However, it is imperative for bank regulators to ensure compliance and prevent abuse of these jurisdictions for illicit purposes.

Cook Islands

Cook Islands: A Haven for Offshore Banking and Asset Protection

Introduction:

In the world of offshore banking, the Cook Islands have emerged as a prominent destination offering a range of benefits for individuals and businesses seeking tax-efficient solutions, asset protection, and privacy. This subchapter explores the various aspects that make the Cook Islands an attractive option for bank regulators and the niches of offshore banking tax havens, digital nomad tax havens, retirement tax havens, cryptocurrency tax havens, asset protection tax havens, estate planning tax havens, high-net-worth individual tax havens, business tax havens, real estate investment tax havens, and privacy-focused tax havens.

1. Tax Advantages:

The Cook Islands have established a favorable tax regime that enables individuals and corporations to optimize their tax liabilities legally. As a tax haven, the jurisdiction imposes no taxes on offshore income, capital gains, or inheritance, making it highly appealing for high-net-worth individuals, businesses, and retirees seeking to minimize their tax burden.

2. Asset Protection and Wealth Preservation:

The Cook Islands' robust asset protection laws are a key draw for individuals looking to safeguard their assets from potential lawsuits or creditors. The jurisdiction offers a unique combination of irrevocable trusts, limited liability companies, and foundations, which provide enhanced protection against legal claims. Bank regulators can explore the jurisdiction's legal framework to understand how these structures can be utilized effectively.

3. Privacy and Confidentiality:

With an unwavering commitment to privacy, the Cook Islands are known for their strict confidentiality laws that safeguard the identity of account holders and ensure the utmost discretion. This feature appeals to individuals seeking to protect their financial affairs and maintain anonymity.

4. Digital Nomad and Retirement Haven:

The Cook Islands offer a serene and idyllic environment that appeals to digital nomads and retirees. Its welcoming policies, low crime rates, and stunning natural beauty make it an attractive destination for individuals seeking a peaceful and tax-efficient lifestyle.

5. Cryptocurrency and Business Opportunities:

The Cook Islands have embraced the growing digital economy, with favorable regulations for businesses involved in cryptocurrencies and fintech. Bank regulators can explore the jurisdiction's licensing framework and understand how it can attract businesses operating in these sectors.

6. Real Estate Investment:

Investors looking to diversify their portfolios can benefit from the Cook Islands' real estate investment opportunities. The jurisdiction boasts a stable property market and attractive investment incentives, making it an appealing option for those seeking to invest in real estate.

Conclusion:

The Cook Islands offer a compelling range of benefits for bank regulators and individuals across various offshore banking niches. Its tax advantages, asset protection laws, privacy provisions, and business opportunities make it an attractive destination for those seeking a tax-efficient, secure, and confidential offshore banking experience. By gaining an understanding of the Cook Islands' unique offerings, bank regulators can assess its regulatory framework and guide their institutions in effectively navigating offshore banking services in this jurisdiction.

Nevis

Nevis: A Premier Offshore Banking and Tax Haven

Introduction:

In the realm of offshore banking, few destinations can match the allure and advantages offered by the Caribbean island of Nevis. With its robust financial services industry, investor-friendly regulations, and attractive tax incentives, Nevis has emerged as a premier choice for individuals and businesses seeking to optimize their offshore banking strategies. In this subchapter, we will explore the key features and benefits that make Nevis an ideal destination for a diverse range of offshore banking needs.

Tax Advantages:

One of the primary reasons individuals and businesses flock to Nevis is its favorable tax environment. As a tax haven, Nevis offers a range of tax incentives, including zero taxes on foreign-source income, capital gains, wealth, and inheritance. This makes it an attractive option for high-net-worth individuals, retirees, and digital nomads looking to minimize their tax obligations while maintaining financial privacy.

Asset Protection and Estate Planning:

Nevis has gained significant recognition for its robust asset protection laws, making it a sought-after jurisdiction for safeguarding wealth and assets. The Nevis Multiform Foundation Act provides a unique structure for protecting assets, shielding them from potential lawsuits, creditors, and other risks. Additionally, the island offers a secure environment for estate planning, allowing individuals to efficiently pass down their wealth to future generations.

Business and Investment Opportunities:

Nevis also provides a favorable environment for businesses and investors. Its well-regulated banking sector, political stability, and business-friendly policies attract entrepreneurs seeking to establish offshore entities. The Nevis Limited Liability Company (LLC) offers flexible and efficient structuring options, providing liability protection and tax advantages for businesses operating internationally. Furthermore, the island's real estate market presents attractive investment opportunities, particularly for those seeking to diversify their portfolios.

Digital Nomad and Cryptocurrency Haven:

Nevis has positioned itself as a digital nomad and cryptocurrency haven, catering to the growing global trend of remote work and digital entrepreneurship. With its reliable internet infrastructure, beautiful landscapes, and welcoming environment, Nevis attracts location-independent professionals seeking a tax-friendly destination to base their operations. Additionally, the island has embraced the rise of cryptocurrencies, offering a supportive regulatory framework for blockchain and digital asset initiatives.

Conclusion:

Nevis, with its favorable tax environment, robust asset protection laws, and business-friendly regulations, has firmly established itself as a leading offshore banking and tax haven. Whether for high-net-worth individuals, retirees, digital nomads, or businesses, Nevis offers a secure and attractive destination to optimize financial strategies and ensure long-term prosperity. As bank regulators, understanding the unique advantages and challenges presented by Nevis will enable you to effectively navigate the offshore banking landscape and provide informed guidance to clients seeking to leverage its benefits.

Belize

Belize: A Diversified Tax Haven Oasis

Located in Central America, Belize has emerged as a premier destination for offshore banking and offers a range of tax advantages to international investors. With its attractive tax policies, stable economy, and strict privacy laws, Belize has become a preferred choice for individuals and businesses seeking to optimize their financial strategies.

For offshore banking tax havens, Belize offers a favorable tax environment. The country imposes no taxes on income earned outside of Belize, including dividends, capital gains, and interest. This allows individuals and businesses to legally reduce their tax liabilities while enjoying the benefits of offshore investments.

Digital nomads, who often face complex tax situations due to their global mobility, can also find solace in Belize. The country offers a special program called the "Qualified Retired Persons Incentive Program" (QRP), which provides a range of tax incentives to retirees and remote workers. Under this program, participants are exempt from taxes on foreign income, imports of personal goods, and capital gains on assets acquired after becoming residents.

Retirement tax havens seekers can find a peaceful and affordable haven in Belize. The country's low cost of living, beautiful landscapes, and warm climate make it an ideal retirement destination. Retirees can take advantage of the QRP program mentioned earlier, ensuring a comfortable and tax-efficient retirement.

Belize is also gaining recognition as a cryptocurrency tax haven. The government has introduced legislation to regulate and promote cryptocurrency-related activities, creating a favorable environment for businesses and individuals involved in the digital currency space. Cryptocurrency investors can benefit from Belize's tax-free status on capital gains, attracting both local and foreign investors.

Furthermore, Belize serves as an asset protection tax haven. The country's International Business Companies (IBCs) provide a secure framework for protecting assets from legal claims, creditors, or other potential risks. The IBCs offer the flexibility of managing assets, including real estate, intellectual property, and financial investments, with utmost privacy and confidentiality.

Estate planning tax havens seekers can also find refuge in Belize. Trusts established in Belize enjoy robust legal protection and allow for seamless transfer of wealth to future generations. The country's trust laws provide a high level of confidentiality, ensuring privacy for individuals and their beneficiaries.

High-net-worth individuals looking to optimize their tax planning can benefit from Belize's progressive tax laws. The country provides various legal structures, such as international trusts and foundations, to help preserve wealth and minimize tax liabilities.

Additionally, Belize serves as a business tax haven, offering a business-friendly environment with low corporate tax rates. International companies can set up their operations in Belize and take advantage of its strategic location, skilled workforce, and competitive cost structure.

Real estate investment tax havens seekers can explore the lucrative opportunities Belize has to offer. The country's stable economy, affordable land prices, and growing tourism industry make it an attractive destination for real estate investments. Investors can benefit from tax incentives, such as the exemption of capital gains tax on the sale of property held for more than three years.

Lastly, Belize is a privacy-focused tax haven. The country has strict confidentiality laws that protect the privacy of individuals and businesses. Belizean banks are known for their commitment to maintaining client confidentiality, making it an excellent choice for those seeking financial privacy.

In conclusion, Belize provides a diverse range of tax advantages and investment opportunities for individuals and businesses in various niches. With its stable economy, favorable tax policies, and commitment to privacy, Belize has firmly established itself as a leading offshore banking tax haven. Bank regulators can benefit from understanding the unique advantages Belize offers to their respective niches, allowing them to effectively regulate and navigate the offshore banking landscape.

Bermuda

Bermuda: A Premier Offshore Banking Destination

Introduction:

In the world of offshore banking, Bermuda holds a prominent position as a premier tax haven. With its favorable tax policies, robust regulatory framework, and attractive investment opportunities, Bermuda has become a preferred destination for various niches, including offshore banking tax havens, digital nomad tax havens, retirement tax havens, cryptocurrency tax havens, asset protection tax havens, estate planning tax havens, high-net-worth individual tax havens, business tax havens, real estate investment tax havens, and privacy-focused tax havens. This subchapter aims to provide bank regulators with an in-depth understanding of Bermuda's offshore banking landscape.

Tax Advantages:

Bermuda's tax regime offers several advantages to individuals and businesses seeking to optimize their financial affairs. Firstly, the jurisdiction has no corporate income tax, making it an attractive destination for businesses looking to minimize their tax liabilities. Additionally, there are no capital gains or withholding taxes, further enhancing its appeal to investors. For individuals, Bermuda does not levy personal income tax, making it an ideal location for high-net-worth individuals seeking to preserve their wealth.

Regulatory Framework:

One of Bermuda's key strengths lies in its robust regulatory framework, which adheres to international standards and best practices. The

Bermuda Monetary Authority (BMA) oversees the banking sector and ensures compliance with anti-money laundering (AML) and know-your-customer (KYC) regulations. Bank regulators can take comfort in Bermuda's commitment to maintaining a secure and stable financial system.

Investment Opportunities:

Bermuda offers a diverse range of investment opportunities, making it an attractive destination for offshore banking. From real estate to cryptocurrencies, individuals and businesses can find avenues to grow their wealth. The island's stable economy, strong legal system, and reputation as a global financial hub make it an ideal location for both traditional and innovative investments.

Privacy and Confidentiality:

In addition to its tax advantages, Bermuda is known for its commitment to privacy and confidentiality. The island's laws ensure that individuals' financial information remains secure and protected. This aspect is particularly appealing to those seeking privacy-focused tax havens, such as high-net-worth individuals and business owners who value discretion.

Conclusion:

Bermuda's position as a premier offshore banking destination is well-established, attracting various niches within the banking industry. Its tax advantages, robust regulatory framework, diverse investment opportunities, and commitment to privacy make it an ideal location for bank regulators to monitor and understand. By comprehending Bermuda's offshore banking landscape, regulators can effectively navigate the complexities of this jurisdiction and ensure the integrity and stability of the financial system.

Isle of Man

Isle of Man: A Hub for Offshore Banking and Financial Services

The Isle of Man is a small self-governing British Crown dependency located in the Irish Sea. Renowned for its robust regulatory framework and favorable tax regime, the island has emerged as a leading destination for offshore banking and financial services. This subchapter explores the unique features and advantages that make the Isle of Man an attractive option for individuals and businesses seeking offshore banking solutions.

1. Offshore banking tax havens: The Isle of Man offers a competitive tax environment with low corporate tax rates and no capital gains or inheritance taxes. This makes it an ideal jurisdiction for individuals and businesses looking to minimize their tax liabilities legally.

2. Digital nomad tax havens: With its excellent infrastructure and reliable internet connectivity, the Isle of Man is an attractive destination for digital nomads. The island's flexible residency and tax laws allow remote workers to benefit from its favorable tax regime while enjoying a high quality of life.

3. Retirement tax havens: The Isle of Man offers a range of retirement solutions, including internationally recognized pension schemes. Retirees can take advantage of the island's tax-efficient environment and enjoy their golden years in a secure and beautiful location.

4. Cryptocurrency tax havens: The Isle of Man has positioned itself as a global center for cryptocurrency and blockchain technology. Its forward-thinking regulatory approach provides a supportive environment for businesses operating in this rapidly growing industry.

5. Asset protection tax havens: The Isle of Man has a long history of providing robust asset protection services. Its legal system offers

strong creditor protection, ensuring that individuals and businesses can safeguard their wealth and assets.

6. Estate planning tax havens: The Isle of Man offers a range of trust and estate planning structures that provide individuals with control and flexibility over their assets. These structures, combined with the island's favorable tax regime, make it an attractive jurisdiction for estate planning purposes.

7. High-net-worth individual tax havens: The Isle of Man has a well-established reputation as a destination for high-net-worth individuals. Its sophisticated financial services sector, coupled with its tax advantages, attracts wealthy individuals looking for wealth management and investment opportunities.

8. Business tax havens: The Isle of Man provides a supportive environment for businesses, with streamlined company formation processes, access to international markets, and a favorable tax regime. It is particularly attractive for businesses engaged in international trade and e-commerce.

9. Real estate investment tax havens: The Isle of Man offers a stable and secure real estate market, making it an attractive destination for property investors. The absence of capital gains tax and inheritance tax further enhances the appeal of real estate investments on the island.

10. Privacy-focused tax havens: The Isle of Man has a strong commitment to data protection and privacy. Its regulatory framework ensures the confidentiality of banking and financial information, making it an appealing jurisdiction for individuals and businesses seeking privacy in their financial affairs.

In conclusion, the Isle of Man's favorable tax regime, robust regulatory framework, and commitment to privacy make it a top choice for individuals and businesses seeking offshore banking and financial services. Its advantages extend to various niches, including offshore banking tax havens, cryptocurrency tax havens, retirement tax havens, and more. Bank regulators should be aware of the unique features and benefits of the Isle of Man to effectively regulate and oversee offshore banking activities in this jurisdiction.

Legal Frameworks and Trust Structures in Asset Protection Tax Havens

Introduction:

In this subchapter, we will delve into the legal frameworks and trust structures that exist in asset protection tax havens. As bank regulators, it is essential to understand the intricacies of these jurisdictions to effectively regulate offshore banking activities, especially in the context of asset protection.

Understanding Asset Protection Tax Havens:

Asset protection tax havens are jurisdictions that offer favorable legal environments and robust trust structures to safeguard assets from potential risks and liabilities. These havens attract various niche groups, including high-net-worth individuals, business owners, digital nomads, retirees, and cryptocurrency enthusiasts, seeking to protect and grow their wealth.

Legal Frameworks:

Asset protection tax havens typically have well-established legal frameworks that provide favorable tax incentives, strong privacy laws, and comprehensive asset protection statutes. These jurisdictions often have low or zero tax rates on offshore income, capital gains, and inheritance, providing individuals and businesses with substantial tax advantages.

Trust Structures:

Trust structures play a vital role in asset protection tax havens. These structures are legal arrangements that allow individuals to transfer assets to a trustee who holds and manages them on behalf of the beneficiaries. Trusts provide a level of flexibility, privacy, and protection against potential creditors, lawsuits, and other risks.

Common types of trusts found in asset protection tax havens include discretionary trusts, purpose trusts, and asset protection trusts. Each trust has its unique features and advantages, allowing individuals to tailor their asset protection strategies to their specific needs.

Regulatory Oversight:

As bank regulators, it is crucial to ensure that the legal frameworks and trust structures in asset protection tax havens are effectively regulated. This includes ensuring compliance with international standards, preventing money laundering, and maintaining the integrity of the financial system.

Conclusion:

Understanding the legal frameworks and trust structures in asset protection tax havens is of utmost importance for bank regulators. By comprehending the nuances of these jurisdictions, regulators can effectively monitor and regulate offshore banking activities, ensuring compliance, and maintaining the integrity of the financial system. It is essential to strike a balance between providing favorable environments for legitimate asset protection and preventing illicit activities that may undermine global financial stability.

Offshore Trusts

Offshore Trusts: A Powerful Tool in Offshore Banking

In the ever-evolving landscape of offshore banking tax havens, it is crucial for bank regulators to understand the intricacies of offshore trusts. These unique financial instruments have gained significant popularity among various niches such as digital nomads, retirees, high-net-worth individuals, and those seeking privacy-focused tax havens. In this subchapter, we will explore the key features and benefits of offshore trusts, shedding light on their relevance to different sectors of offshore banking.

One of the primary advantages of offshore trusts is their ability to provide asset protection. By establishing a trust in a reputable tax haven jurisdiction, individuals and businesses can safeguard their wealth from potential creditors, litigations, and other risks. This feature is particularly appealing to high-net-worth individuals, who seek to shield their assets from potential threats.

Furthermore, offshore trusts can play a crucial role in estate planning. In tax havens that offer favorable inheritance laws, individuals can efficiently manage and distribute their wealth to future generations. This aspect is especially relevant for retirees and business owners looking to ensure the smooth transfer of their assets.

For digital nomads and individuals involved in the cryptocurrency market, offshore trusts offer a unique opportunity for tax optimization. By establishing a trust in a cryptocurrency tax haven, individuals can legally minimize their tax liabilities, allowing them to maximize their investment returns. This presents a compelling proposition for those seeking to capitalize on the booming digital currency industry.

In addition to tax optimization, offshore trusts can also serve as a valuable tool for business owners and real estate investors. By structuring their business or investment holdings through a trust in a business tax haven or real estate investment tax haven, individuals can benefit from favorable tax incentives, reduced bureaucracy, and increased privacy.

Lastly, offshore trusts cater to the increasing demand for privacy-focused tax havens. With growing concerns about data security and confidentiality, individuals and businesses are seeking jurisdictions that prioritize privacy. Offshore trusts, in combination with the right tax haven, can provide an ideal solution for those who value their privacy and seek to protect their financial information.

In conclusion, offshore trusts are a powerful tool in the realm of offshore banking. Their versatility and ability to cater to the specific needs of different niches make them an indispensable asset for individuals and businesses alike. By understanding the intricacies of offshore trusts, bank regulators can effectively navigate the complex landscape of offshore banking tax havens, ensuring compliance and promoting the growth of this vital sector.

Limited Liability Companies (LLCs)

In today's globalized economy, the concept of offshore banking has gained significant traction. Offshore tax havens have become popular among various niches, including digital nomads, retirees, cryptocurrency enthusiasts, high-net-worth individuals, and businesses seeking asset protection, estate planning, real estate investment, and privacy. One key legal entity that plays a crucial role in facilitating these financial activities is the Limited Liability Company (LLC).

An LLC is a flexible and versatile business entity structure that combines the benefits of a corporation and a partnership. It provides the owners, known as members, with limited liability protection, shielding their personal assets from the company's debts and liabilities. LLCs have become increasingly popular in offshore banking tax havens for their simplicity, tax advantages, and asset protection features.

For bank regulators overseeing offshore banking tax havens, understanding the intricacies of LLCs is essential. LLCs offer a range of benefits, including flexible management structures, pass-through taxation, and limited compliance requirements. These features make them attractive for businesses operating in various industries, such as real estate, technology, and finance.

LLCs also play a significant role in digital nomad tax havens, catering to individuals whose work is not tied to a specific location. These tax havens offer favorable tax regimes for remote workers, and LLCs allow them to establish a legal presence while enjoying tax benefits and asset protection.

Retirement tax havens often attract individuals seeking financial stability and favorable tax treatment during their golden years. LLCs can be a valuable tool for retirees, allowing them to structure their assets and investments efficiently while minimizing tax liabilities.

Cryptocurrency tax havens have emerged in recent years, offering a favorable regulatory environment for blockchain and digital asset businesses. LLCs provide a suitable legal structure for cryptocurrency ventures, ensuring limited liability while navigating the complexities of this emerging industry.

Asset protection tax havens serve as a safe haven for individuals and businesses looking to safeguard their wealth from potential risks. LLCs in these jurisdictions offer a robust legal framework to shield assets and minimize exposure to litigation.

Estate planning tax havens offer favorable tax treatment for individuals looking to preserve their wealth for future generations. LLCs can be utilized in sophisticated estate planning strategies, ensuring seamless wealth transfer and minimizing estate tax liabilities.

High-net-worth individual tax havens attract wealthy individuals seeking to optimize their tax position and protect their assets. LLCs in these jurisdictions offer a secure vehicle for managing investments, real estate holdings, and business interests.

Business tax havens provide a favorable tax environment for companies looking to minimize their tax burden and optimize their international operations. LLCs offer a simple and efficient structure for businesses, ensuring flexibility and limited liability.

Real estate investment tax havens attract investors looking to capitalize on lucrative property markets while minimizing tax liabilities. LLCs offer a flexible and efficient vehicle for holding and managing real estate assets.

Privacy-focused tax havens cater to individuals and businesses seeking confidentiality and anonymity. LLCs in these jurisdictions provide a high level of privacy protection, ensuring the utmost discretion for financial transactions and asset management.

In conclusion, Limited Liability Companies (LLCs) are a vital component of the offshore banking ecosystem. Their flexibility, simplicity, and asset protection features make them a preferred choice for individuals and businesses across various niches. For bank regulators overseeing offshore tax havens, a comprehensive understanding of LLCs is crucial to ensure effective oversight and regulation of these financial activities.

Foundations

In the realm of offshore banking, foundations play a crucial role in providing a secure and efficient vehicle for individuals and businesses to manage their assets. As bank regulators, it is essential to understand the foundations that underpin the offshore banking industry and their implications for various niches, including offshore banking tax havens, digital nomad tax havens, retirement tax havens, cryptocurrency tax havens, asset protection tax havens, estate planning tax havens, high-net-worth individual tax havens, business tax havens, real estate investment tax havens, and privacy-focused tax havens.

Foundations serve as legal entities that hold and manage assets on behalf of individuals or organizations. They offer a range of benefits, including tax advantages, asset protection, and estate planning opportunities. In offshore banking tax havens, foundations are particularly popular due to their ability to minimize tax liabilities legally. Bank regulators must be familiar with the various tax havens and their specific regulations to effectively oversee the operations of offshore banks operating within these jurisdictions.

For digital nomads, who often lead location-independent lifestyles, tax havens provide an attractive proposition. Foundations can serve as an effective tool for managing their finances, ensuring compliance with tax laws, and optimizing their tax positions. Retirement tax havens, on the other hand, offer retirees the opportunity to enjoy their golden years while minimizing their tax burden. Understanding the intricacies of foundations within retirement tax havens is essential for regulators to ensure the protection of retirees' assets.

The rise of cryptocurrencies has led to the emergence of cryptocurrency tax havens, where foundations play a significant role in managing and protecting digital assets. Regulators need to stay updated on the ever-evolving landscape of cryptocurrencies and the associated tax implications to effectively regulate offshore banks operating in these jurisdictions.

Asset protection and estate planning tax havens offer individuals and businesses the ability to safeguard their wealth and plan for future generations. High-net-worth individuals, with their complex financial structures, require meticulous oversight to ensure compliance with regulations and prevent illicit activities. Business tax havens, real estate investment tax havens, and privacy-focused tax havens also rely on robust foundation structures to facilitate their respective niches.

In this subchapter, we will delve into the foundations that form the backbone of the offshore banking industry. We will explore their legal frameworks, tax implications, and the role they play in various niches. By understanding the foundations, bank regulators can effectively ensure the integrity, transparency, and stability of offshore banking operations in these tax havens, ultimately fostering a secure and regulated environment for all stakeholders involved.

Chapter 7: Estate Planning Tax Havens

Importance of Estate Planning in Offshore Tax Havens

In the world of offshore banking and tax havens, estate planning plays a crucial role for individuals and businesses alike. Estate planning is the process of organizing and managing one's assets to ensure their seamless transfer and protection upon death or incapacitation. While estate planning is important in any jurisdiction, offshore tax havens offer unique advantages and considerations that make it even more critical.

For bank regulators overseeing offshore banking tax havens, understanding the importance of estate planning is essential. Offshore tax havens attract a diverse range of clients, including digital nomads, retirees, high-net-worth individuals, cryptocurrency users, and businesses seeking favorable tax environments. Each niche has its specific estate planning needs, but they all share a common goal: preserving and optimizing their assets.

One of the primary benefits of offshore tax havens is the potential to minimize or even eliminate estate taxes. By strategically structuring assets and leveraging legal mechanisms available in these jurisdictions, individuals can pass on their wealth without exorbitant tax burdens. Bank regulators need to be aware of the intricacies of these estate planning strategies to ensure compliance with international tax laws and prevent potential abuse.

Moreover, offshore tax havens offer privacy and asset protection advantages that make estate planning even more appealing. These jurisdictions often have robust laws that safeguard assets from creditors, lawsuits, and other potential threats. By incorporating offshore trusts and foundations into their estate plans, individuals can shield their assets from prying eyes and ensure their intended beneficiaries inherit their wealth according to their wishes.

In the realm of cryptocurrency, estate planning becomes even more critical. Cryptocurrency tax havens, with their lenient regulations and favorable tax treatment, attract many investors and traders. However, the unique nature of digital assets necessitates careful estate planning to ensure their secure transfer and prevent loss due to mishandling or lack of access. Bank regulators must stay abreast of the evolving landscape of cryptocurrencies and their implications for estate planning in offshore tax havens.

Overall, estate planning in offshore tax havens is a complex but vital aspect of offshore banking. Bank regulators must familiarize themselves with the intricacies of estate planning strategies employed by different niches, including digital nomads, retirees, high-net-worth individuals, cryptocurrency users, and businesses. By understanding and overseeing these estate planning practices, regulators can ensure the integrity and compliance of offshore banking tax havens while protecting both the interests of clients and the integrity of the financial system.

Prominent Estate Planning Tax Havens

Estate planning is a critical aspect of financial management that involves the transfer of assets from one generation to the next. For high-net-worth individuals, it becomes imperative to explore tax-efficient strategies to protect and preserve their wealth. This subchapter delves into the world of prominent estate planning tax havens, which offer attractive opportunities for individuals looking to optimize their tax liabilities.

Offshore banking tax havens have long been recognized as a popular choice for estate planning due to their favorable tax regimes. Countries such as Switzerland, the Cayman Islands, and the British Virgin Islands have established themselves as leading destinations for individuals seeking to protect their assets and minimize their tax burdens. These jurisdictions offer a range of structures, including trusts and foundations, which provide flexibility and confidentiality for estate planning purposes.

Digital nomad tax havens are gaining prominence in the modern era, as individuals increasingly embrace remote work and digital entrepreneurship. Countries like Estonia, Portugal, and Malta have introduced attractive tax incentives for digital nomads, making them appealing options for estate planning. These jurisdictions provide favorable tax rates and flexible residency requirements, allowing individuals to structure their estates in a tax-efficient manner.

Retirement tax havens are another category of tax havens that cater specifically to retirees. Countries like Panama, Costa Rica, and Belize offer attractive retirement programs, providing retirees with significant tax benefits and financial incentives. These jurisdictions allow retirees to structure their estates in a way that minimizes taxes while ensuring a comfortable retirement lifestyle.

Cryptocurrency tax havens have emerged as a niche area within estate planning, given the growing popularity of digital currencies. Countries like Malta, Switzerland, and Bermuda have established themselves as cryptocurrency-friendly jurisdictions, offering favorable tax regimes for individuals engaged in cryptocurrency investments. These tax havens provide a secure and regulated environment for estate planning involving digital assets.

Asset protection tax havens are particularly appealing for individuals seeking to safeguard their wealth from potential lawsuits or creditors. Jurisdictions like the Cook Islands, Nevis, and the Isle of Man offer robust asset protection laws, making them attractive options for estate planning purposes. These tax havens provide a level of legal protection that ensures the preservation of assets for future generations.

In conclusion, prominent estate planning tax havens offer a range of opportunities for high-net-worth individuals to optimize their tax liabilities and protect their assets. Whether it is offshore banking tax havens, digital nomad tax havens, or retirement tax havens, individuals can leverage these jurisdictions to structure their estates in a tax-efficient manner. Moreover, with the rise of cryptocurrency and the need for asset protection, estate planning tax havens have expanded to cater to these specific needs. As bank regulators, understanding the dynamics of these tax havens is essential to effectively regulate offshore banking activities and ensure compliance with international tax laws.

Switzerland

Switzerland: The Epitome of Offshore Banking Tax Havens

When it comes to offshore banking tax havens, Switzerland is often the first country that comes to mind. Renowned for its political stability, strong financial system, and strict adherence to banking secrecy laws, Switzerland has long been a preferred destination for individuals and businesses seeking to protect their assets and minimize their tax liabilities.

For bank regulators, understanding the intricacies of Switzerland's offshore banking landscape is crucial. With its reputation as a global financial center, Switzerland attracts a diverse range of clients, including digital nomads, retirees, high-net-worth individuals, and businesses looking for privacy and favorable tax treatment.

Switzerland offers a wide array of services tailored to different niches. Digital nomads, for instance, can benefit from Switzerland's attractive tax regime for foreign-sourced income, allowing them to enjoy the perks of this beautiful country while minimizing their tax burden.

Retirement tax havens in Switzerland provide a safe and stable environment for retirees to preserve and grow their wealth, with attractive tax incentives and a high quality of life.

Cryptocurrency tax havens have also emerged in Switzerland, capitalizing on the country's favorable regulatory environment for digital assets. The Swiss government's progressive approach towards cryptocurrencies has attracted numerous blockchain companies and investors, making Switzerland a hub for this emerging industry.

Furthermore, Switzerland's asset protection tax havens provide a secure environment for individuals and businesses to shield their assets from potential legal claims or creditors. Estate planning tax havens in Switzerland offer sophisticated wealth management solutions, ensuring smooth succession planning and minimizing inheritance taxes.

For high-net-worth individuals, Switzerland's private banking sector is second to none. With its long-standing tradition of preserving wealth and providing personalized services, Swiss private banks cater to the specific needs of affluent clients, offering a wide range of investment options and financial instruments.

Business tax havens in Switzerland are also highly sought after, given the country's favorable corporate tax rates and business-friendly environment. Real estate investment tax havens are equally attractive, with Switzerland's stable property market and potential for capital appreciation.

Lastly, privacy-focused tax havens in Switzerland remain a key draw for individuals and businesses seeking discretion and confidentiality. Swiss banks are known for their stringent client identification procedures and commitment to banking secrecy, ensuring utmost privacy for account holders.

In conclusion, Switzerland stands as the epitome of offshore banking tax havens, offering a diverse range of services tailored to the needs of various niches. Bank regulators must familiarize themselves with the intricacies of Switzerland's offshore banking sector to effectively navigate this complex landscape and ensure compliance with international regulations. Understanding the nuances of Switzerland's offerings to digital nomads, retirees, cryptocurrency enthusiasts, asset protectors, estate planners, high-net-worth individuals, businesses, real estate investors, and privacy seekers is essential to effectively regulate the offshore banking industry in this global financial center.

Liechtenstein

Liechtenstein: A Premier Offshore Banking and Tax Haven

Nestled between Switzerland and Austria, Liechtenstein stands as a renowned offshore banking jurisdiction, offering a wide range of benefits for individuals and businesses seeking to optimize their financial strategies. As bank regulators, it is essential to understand the unique opportunities and challenges presented by Liechtenstein to effectively navigate this thriving offshore banking landscape.

Offshore Banking Tax Havens: Liechtenstein has long been recognized as a premier offshore banking destination due to its favorable tax environment. With low corporate tax rates and an attractive tax regime for high-net-worth individuals, Liechtenstein provides an ideal platform for tax optimization and wealth preservation.

Digital Nomad Tax Havens: In the era of remote work and digital nomadism, Liechtenstein emerges as an attractive option for individuals seeking tax-efficient solutions. Its flexible residency programs and favorable tax policies for non-domiciled individuals make it an ideal destination for digital nomads looking to minimize their tax liabilities.

Retirement Tax Havens: Liechtenstein offers a secure and stable environment for retirees looking to protect their assets and optimize their retirement savings. With its robust financial sector and comprehensive wealth management services, Liechtenstein provides a range of investment opportunities for retirees seeking to grow and safeguard their wealth.

Cryptocurrency Tax Havens: Liechtenstein has embraced the blockchain revolution, positioning itself as a cryptocurrency-friendly jurisdiction. Its regulatory framework, including the groundbreaking Blockchain Act, fosters innovation and provides a secure environment for businesses and individuals involved in the crypto space.

Asset Protection Tax Havens: For those seeking to shield their assets from potential risks and legal uncertainties, Liechtenstein offers a range of asset protection solutions. Its trust and foundation structures provide a robust legal framework for safeguarding wealth and ensuring confidentiality.

Estate Planning Tax Havens: Liechtenstein's trust and foundation laws also make it an attractive destination for estate planning purposes. Its efficient wealth transfer mechanisms, combined with favorable tax treatment, allow individuals to preserve and pass on their assets to future generations seamlessly.

High-Net-Worth Individual Tax Havens: With its sophisticated financial services industry, Liechtenstein caters to the needs of high-net-worth individuals seeking personalized and comprehensive wealth management solutions. Its private banking sector offers a wide range of investment options and tailored services to meet the unique requirements of wealthy clients.

Business Tax Havens: Liechtenstein's business-friendly environment, coupled with its advantageous tax policies, makes it an ideal destination for entrepreneurs and businesses. Its strong legal system, political stability, and access to European markets create an attractive ecosystem for establishing and operating businesses.

Real Estate Investment Tax Havens: Liechtenstein's real estate market presents lucrative opportunities for investors looking to diversify their portfolios. With its stable property market and attractive tax incentives, Liechtenstein offers a favorable environment for real estate investment.

Privacy-Focused Tax Havens: Liechtenstein has a long-standing tradition of respecting and safeguarding individuals' privacy. Its commitment to confidentiality, combined with its robust legal framework, makes it a sought-after destination for those seeking privacy-focused financial solutions.

In conclusion, Liechtenstein's appeal as an offshore banking and tax haven is evident across various niches, offering a range of advantages for bank regulators and their respective areas of interest. By understanding the unique opportunities and challenges presented by Liechtenstein, regulators can effectively navigate the intricacies of this thriving offshore banking jurisdiction.

Isle of Man

Isle of Man: A Premier Offshore Banking Jurisdiction

Introduction:

The Isle of Man is a renowned offshore banking jurisdiction that offers a wide range of benefits for individuals and businesses seeking to optimize their financial affairs. With its robust regulatory framework, political stability, and attractive tax incentives, the Isle of Man has become a preferred choice for offshore banking activities. This subchapter will delve into the various aspects that make the Isle of Man an ideal destination for both personal and corporate offshore banking endeavors.

Overview of the Isle of Man:

Located in the Irish Sea, the Isle of Man is a self-governing British Crown Dependency with a thriving economy built on financial services, including offshore banking. Its strategic location, between the United Kingdom and Ireland, provides easy access to the European market, making it an attractive choice for international investors.

Regulatory Environment:

The Isle of Man boasts a well-developed regulatory system that emphasizes transparency, integrity, and investor protection. The Financial Services Authority (FSA) is the primary regulatory body responsible for overseeing banking activities, ensuring compliance with international standards, such as those set by the Financial Action Task Force (FATF) and the Organisation for Economic Co-operation and Development (OECD).

Tax Advantages:

One of the key attractions of the Isle of Man is its favorable tax regime. While the jurisdiction levies corporate tax at a standard rate, it offers various incentives, including zero or reduced rates for certain types of offshore activities. This makes it an appealing choice for businesses seeking to optimize their tax liabilities while maintaining compliance with international tax regulations.

Privacy and Confidentiality:

The Isle of Man places a strong emphasis on client confidentiality, making it an attractive destination for individuals seeking privacy-focused offshore banking solutions. The jurisdiction has robust data protection laws that safeguard the privacy of clients, providing peace of mind for those who value discretion.

Innovation and Technology:

The Isle of Man has embraced digital transformation, positioning itself as a leader in the fintech industry. As a result, it has become a preferred choice for digital nomads and cryptocurrency enthusiasts looking for tax-efficient solutions. The jurisdiction offers a supportive environment for innovative financial technologies, fostering growth and attracting talent from around the world.

Conclusion:

The Isle of Man stands out as a premier offshore banking jurisdiction, catering to a diverse range of banking needs. Whether it is for asset protection, estate planning, or business expansion, the Isle of Man offers a compelling combination of regulatory strength, tax advantages, privacy protections, and technological innovation. Bank regulators should be aware of the benefits and challenges associated with the Isle of Man to effectively regulate offshore banking activities and ensure compliance with international standards.

Monaco

Monaco: A Haven for Offshore Banking and Financial Privacy

Monaco, a small principality located on the French Riviera, has long been renowned for its glamorous lifestyle, luxurious resorts, and prestigious events like the Monaco Grand Prix. However, beyond its reputation as a playground for the rich and famous, Monaco also offers a highly attractive offshore banking environment that caters to a diverse range of niches, such as offshore banking tax havens, digital nomad tax havens, retirement tax havens, cryptocurrency tax havens, asset protection tax havens, estate planning tax havens, high-net-worth individual tax havens, business tax havens, real estate investment tax havens, and privacy-focused tax havens.

Monaco's appeal as an offshore banking jurisdiction stems from its favorable financial regulations and tax policies. Bank regulators seeking to understand the intricacies of offshore banking will find that Monaco provides a robust framework for banking institutions to operate while ensuring the utmost privacy and confidentiality for their clients. The principality's banking sector adheres to strict anti-money laundering and know-your-customer protocols, ensuring the integrity and transparency of financial transactions.

For digital nomads and individuals seeking tax efficiency, Monaco offers an attractive proposition. With no personal income tax and no capital gains tax, Monaco has become a favored destination for those looking to preserve their wealth and maximize their earnings. Additionally, Monaco's residency requirements are flexible, allowing individuals to establish tax residency without significant physical presence, making it an ideal choice for those leading a location-independent lifestyle.

Retirement tax havens are also well-served by Monaco's offerings. The principality provides a stable and secure environment for retirees, with a high standard of living, excellent healthcare facilities, and a thriving expatriate community. Coupled with its tax advantages, Monaco becomes an appealing option for retirees looking to enjoy their golden years in a financially advantageous setting.

Cryptocurrency enthusiasts and investors will find Monaco to be an attractive tax haven. With its friendly regulatory environment and lack of capital gains tax, Monaco has become a hub for cryptocurrency businesses and individuals seeking to protect their assets and optimize their tax liabilities.

Furthermore, Monaco offers a range of services for asset protection, estate planning, and wealth management. Its robust legal system and sophisticated financial institutions make it an ideal jurisdiction for safeguarding assets, planning for future generations, and optimizing tax liabilities within the bounds of the law.

For high-net-worth individuals, Monaco provides a haven for wealth preservation and growth. With its diverse investment opportunities, including real estate investment tax havens, individuals can benefit from the principality's stable economy and attractive returns.

In conclusion, Monaco's allure as an offshore banking jurisdiction extends to a wide range of niches within the financial sector. Bank regulators seeking to understand and navigate the intricacies of offshore banking will find Monaco to be an essential case study. Its favorable financial regulations, tax advantages, and commitment to privacy make it a true haven for offshore banking and financial planning across various niches, including offshore banking tax havens, digital nomad tax havens, retirement tax havens, cryptocurrency tax havens, asset protection tax havens, estate planning tax havens, high-net-worth individual tax havens, business tax havens, real estate investment tax havens, and privacy-focused tax havens.

Jersey

Jersey: A Premier Offshore Banking Tax Haven

Introduction:

In the world of offshore banking tax havens, Jersey stands out as a premier destination for individuals and businesses seeking financial privacy, asset protection, and tax optimization. Located in the English Channel, this self-governing dependency of the British Crown offers a range of benefits that cater to the diverse needs of bank regulators and clients. This subchapter explores why Jersey is a popular choice among offshore banking tax havens, and how it serves the specific niches of bank regulators and various individuals and businesses.

Benefits for Bank Regulators:

As bank regulators, you play a vital role in supervising financial institutions and ensuring compliance. Jersey offers a transparent and well-regulated financial system, providing you with a high level of confidence in the jurisdiction. The Jersey Financial Services Commission (JFSC) oversees the industry and enforces strict anti-money laundering (AML) and know your customer (KYC) regulations, ensuring the integrity of the banking sector.

Offshore Banking Tax Haven for Various Niches:

1. Digital Nomad Tax Havens:

Jersey's flexible residency laws and attractive tax regime make it an ideal destination for digital nomads seeking tax optimization while enjoying a high standard of living. With no capital gains tax, wealth tax, or inheritance tax, it offers individuals the opportunity to maximize their income and preserve their wealth.

2. Retirement Tax Havens:

The island's peaceful environment, excellent healthcare system, and favorable tax policies make Jersey an appealing option for retirees looking to enjoy their golden years. The absence of capital gains tax and low income tax rates ensure a comfortable retirement without unnecessary financial burdens.

3. Cryptocurrency Tax Havens:

Jersey has positioned itself as a cryptocurrency-friendly jurisdiction by introducing a robust regulatory framework for digital assets. Bank regulators can benefit from the island's expertise in blockchain technology and its supportive environment for cryptocurrency businesses, attracting investors and fostering innovation.

4. Asset Protection Tax Havens:

With its strong legal system and trust legislation, Jersey is a trusted jurisdiction for asset protection. Its laws provide individuals and businesses with a secure environment for safeguarding their wealth from potential risks and creditors.

Conclusion:

Jersey's reputation as a premier offshore banking tax haven makes it an attractive choice for bank regulators and a wide range of clients. Whether you are seeking financial privacy, tax optimization, asset protection, or a conducive environment for your business, Jersey offers a robust and well-regulated framework that caters to your specific needs. By understanding the unique advantages that Jersey provides, bank regulators can effectively navigate the world of offshore banking and guide their clients towards a secure and prosperous financial future.

Estate Planning Tools and Techniques in Tax Havens

In the realm of offshore banking, tax havens have become synonymous with attractive opportunities for individuals seeking various financial benefits. One aspect that often goes hand in hand with offshore banking is estate planning. By strategically utilizing the right tools and techniques available in tax havens, individuals can ensure the smooth transfer of assets and wealth to their beneficiaries while minimizing tax obligations. This subchapter aims to provide bank regulators with an overview of the estate planning tools and techniques commonly employed in tax havens, catering to a wide range of niches including digital nomads, retirees, cryptocurrency enthusiasts, high-net-worth individuals, businesses, real estate investors, and those seeking privacy-focused solutions.

One of the most widely used estate planning tools in tax havens is the establishment of trusts. Trusts offer a range of benefits, including asset protection, tax efficiency, and the ability to pass on wealth to future generations. Tax havens often provide favorable trust legislation, allowing individuals to create irrevocable trusts, discretionary trusts, or even offshore private foundations, depending on their specific needs. These structures can not only help individuals preserve and grow their wealth but also provide a shield against potential creditors or legal challenges.

For digital nomads and retirees seeking tax-efficient solutions, tax havens can offer residency programs that provide significant tax advantages. By becoming residents of these jurisdictions, individuals can benefit from lower income tax rates or even zero taxation on foreign income. This can be particularly beneficial for individuals who earn income through online businesses or remote work arrangements.

Cryptocurrency enthusiasts can take advantage of tax havens that embrace digital currencies. These jurisdictions often offer favorable regulations, allowing for tax-free or low-tax treatment of cryptocurrency transactions. By utilizing these tax havens, individuals can safeguard their wealth and potentially avoid substantial tax liabilities associated with cryptocurrency investments.

Asset protection is another critical aspect of estate planning, and tax havens excel in this area. By structuring assets within legal entities such as corporations or limited liability companies in tax havens, individuals can enjoy enhanced protection against potential lawsuits, creditors, or even government seizures.

Lastly, tax havens also offer various estate planning tools for high-net-worth individuals, businesses, real estate investors, and privacy-focused individuals. These tools may include family offices, private banking services, offshore company formations, real estate investment structures, or the use of nominee services to ensure utmost confidentiality.

In conclusion, understanding and utilizing estate planning tools and techniques in tax havens can provide individuals with invaluable benefits, ranging from tax efficiency to asset protection. As bank regulators, it is crucial to be aware of these practices to ensure the integrity and transparency of the offshore banking industry while balancing the needs of the individuals and businesses that utilize these services.

Trusts and Foundations

In the world of offshore banking, trusts and foundations play a vital role in providing individuals and businesses with a secure and efficient means of managing their wealth. This subchapter is dedicated to exploring the intricacies of trusts and foundations, their benefits, and their relevance to various niches within the offshore banking industry.

For bank regulators, understanding the dynamics of trusts and foundations is essential, as these structures often serve as vehicles for tax optimization and asset protection. By comprehending the intricacies of these entities, regulators can ensure compliance with relevant laws and regulations, while also facilitating a transparent and accountable offshore banking sector.

Trusts are widely recognized as effective tools for estate planning, privacy protection, and asset management. They allow individuals to transfer their assets to a separate legal entity, managed by a trustee, for the benefit of designated beneficiaries. Trusts offer a high level of confidentiality and can be used in various contexts, such as retirement planning, real estate investment, and business succession.

Foundations, on the other hand, are similar to trusts but carry distinct characteristics. They are established as legal entities and often serve philanthropic or charitable purposes. However, foundations can also be used for asset protection and estate planning, particularly in the case of high-net-worth individuals seeking to safeguard their wealth for future generations.

From the perspective of offshore banking tax havens, trusts and foundations play a crucial role in attracting individuals and businesses seeking favorable tax regimes. By utilizing these structures, individuals can legally reduce their tax liabilities while maintaining the utmost privacy and asset protection. Bank regulators must carefully monitor the operations of trusts and foundations to prevent abuse and ensure compliance with international tax standards.

Digital nomads, cryptocurrency enthusiasts, and those involved in the global gig economy can benefit from trusts and foundations in their pursuit of tax optimization and asset protection. These structures provide a secure and flexible platform for managing income earned across multiple jurisdictions, minimizing tax burdens, and safeguarding wealth.

For retirees and individuals planning their estates, trusts and foundations can offer peace of mind by allowing for efficient wealth transfer, ensuring the financial wellbeing of future generations. Additionally, trusts and foundations can be utilized by high-net-worth individuals looking to protect their assets from potential legal risks or creditor claims.

In conclusion, trusts and foundations are indispensable tools within the offshore banking industry, catering to a diverse range of niches. Bank regulators must possess a comprehensive understanding of these structures to effectively regulate and supervise the offshore banking sector, ensuring compliance, transparency, and accountability. By striking the right balance between facilitating legitimate financial activities and preventing illicit practices, regulators can contribute to the growth and stability of offshore banking tax havens, digital nomad tax havens, retirement tax havens, cryptocurrency tax havens, asset protection tax havens, estate planning tax havens, high-net-worth individual tax havens, business tax havens, real estate investment tax havens, and privacy-focused tax havens.

Inheritance Laws and Taxation

In the realm of offshore banking, understanding inheritance laws and taxation is of utmost importance. This subchapter aims to provide bank regulators with comprehensive insights into the complex landscape of inheritance laws and taxation applicable to various niches within offshore banking, including offshore banking tax havens, digital nomad tax havens, retirement tax havens, cryptocurrency tax havens, asset protection tax havens, estate planning tax havens, high-net-worth individual tax havens, business tax havens, real estate investment tax havens, and privacy-focused tax havens.

Inheritance laws and taxation play a significant role in determining the transfer of assets and wealth from one generation to the next. Different offshore jurisdictions have varying laws and tax regimes that impact the distribution of estates and the associated tax liabilities. Bank regulators must be well-versed in these laws to effectively regulate offshore banking activities and ensure compliance with relevant regulations.

Offshore banking tax havens, known for their favorable tax environments, attract individuals and businesses seeking to optimize their tax obligations. Bank regulators need to understand the inheritance laws and taxation policies in these jurisdictions to monitor and regulate the flow of funds effectively. Likewise, digital nomad tax havens, retirement tax havens, and cryptocurrency tax havens have their own unique considerations when it comes to inheritance laws and taxation. Regulators must stay updated on these evolving niches to ensure the integrity of offshore banking systems.

Asset protection tax havens and estate planning tax havens provide individuals with options for safeguarding their wealth and efficiently passing it on to future generations. Bank regulators must comprehend the legal and tax frameworks governing these niches to effectively oversee asset protection strategies and estate planning activities.

Furthermore, high-net-worth individual tax havens, business tax havens, real estate investment tax havens, and privacy-focused tax havens have their own nuances when it comes to inheritance laws and taxation. Bank regulators must possess a deep understanding of these niches to effectively monitor and regulate the financial activities of high-net-worth individuals, businesses, real estate investors, and individuals seeking privacy-focused financial solutions.

In conclusion, inheritance laws and taxation are critical components of offshore banking. Bank regulators must have a comprehensive understanding of these laws and tax regimes to effectively regulate offshore banking activities within various niches. By staying informed and up-to-date on the intricacies of inheritance laws and taxation, regulators can ensure the integrity and stability of offshore banking systems, ultimately benefiting both the industry and its clients.

Probate and Estate Administration

In the realm of offshore banking, understanding the intricacies of probate and estate administration is crucial for bank regulators. This subchapter delves into the various aspects of managing estates and navigating probate procedures in the context of different tax havens. By providing an overview of the key considerations and challenges, this resource aims to equip bank regulators with the necessary knowledge to effectively regulate offshore banking activities related to estate planning and administration.

Estate administration in offshore banking tax havens is a multifaceted process that involves the collection, management, and distribution of assets belonging to a deceased individual. This subchapter explores the unique characteristics and legal frameworks of tax havens, such as digital nomad tax havens, retirement tax havens, cryptocurrency tax havens, asset protection tax havens, estate planning tax havens, high-net-worth individual tax havens, business tax havens, real estate investment tax havens, and privacy-focused tax havens.

Bank regulators will gain insights into the specific estate planning strategies employed in these tax havens, including the utilization of trusts, foundations, and other legal entities to protect assets and minimize tax obligations. Understanding the intricacies of these structures is essential for effectively regulating offshore banking activities and ensuring compliance.

Moreover, this subchapter addresses the challenges associated with cross-border estate administration. Given the global nature of offshore banking, bank regulators must be well-versed in the complexities of managing estates that involve multiple jurisdictions. The subchapter provides guidance on navigating potential conflicts of laws, coordinating with foreign authorities, and facilitating the transfer of assets across borders.

Additionally, this resource highlights the importance of upholding transparency and preventing financial crimes in the context of estate administration. Bank regulators will gain insights into the potential risks associated with offshore banking activities, including money laundering, tax evasion, and fraud. By implementing robust regulatory frameworks, bank regulators can mitigate these risks and ensure the integrity and stability of the offshore banking sector.

In conclusion, probate and estate administration are critical components of offshore banking activities. This subchapter equips bank regulators with the necessary knowledge and tools to effectively regulate estate planning and administration in various tax havens. By understanding the unique characteristics, legal frameworks, and challenges associated with offshore estate administration, bank regulators can ensure compliance, transparency, and the prevention of financial crimes in the realm of offshore banking.

Chapter 8: High-Net-Worth Individual Tax Havens

Introduction to High-Net-Worth Individual (HNWI) Tax Havens

In the world of offshore banking, High-Net-Worth Individuals (HNWIs) often seek tax havens to optimize their financial strategies and protect their wealth. This subchapter aims to provide bank regulators with an introduction to HNWI tax havens, exploring various niches such as offshore banking, digital nomad tax havens, retirement tax havens, cryptocurrency tax havens, asset protection tax havens, estate planning tax havens, business tax havens, real estate investment tax havens, and privacy-focused tax havens.

Offshore banking tax havens have long been popular among HNWIs due to their favorable tax regimes and strict confidentiality laws. By moving their funds to these jurisdictions, HNWIs can enjoy reduced tax liabilities and enhanced privacy. However, it is crucial for bank regulators to ensure that these tax havens comply with international regulations and prevent money laundering or illicit activities.

Digital nomad tax havens have emerged as a niche in recent years, catering to individuals who work remotely while traveling the world. These tax havens offer advantages such as low personal income tax rates, flexible residency requirements, and digital infrastructure to support remote work. Bank regulators must monitor these jurisdictions to ensure they strike a balance between attracting digital nomads and maintaining tax transparency.

Retirement tax havens provide attractive options for HNWIs seeking a comfortable retirement while minimizing their tax burden. These havens typically offer favorable tax rates on pension income or provide tax exemptions for retirees. Bank regulators must ensure that these jurisdictions have robust retirement programs in place and comply with international tax standards.

Cryptocurrency tax havens have gained prominence with the rise of digital currencies. These havens offer tax advantages for cryptocurrency investors, including exemptions on capital gains or reduced tax rates. Bank regulators must monitor these jurisdictions to prevent money laundering, protect investors, and ensure transparency in cryptocurrency transactions.

Asset protection tax havens cater to HNWIs seeking to safeguard their assets from potential legal claims or creditors. These havens provide strong asset protection laws, including trusts and foundations, which shield assets from litigation. Bank regulators need to ensure that these jurisdictions maintain sufficient legal frameworks to prevent misuse or abuse of asset protection structures.

Estate planning tax havens offer advantages for HNWIs planning for the transfer of their wealth to future generations. These havens provide favorable inheritance tax regimes, trusts, and other legal mechanisms to facilitate efficient wealth transfer. Bank regulators should ensure that these jurisdictions have robust estate planning frameworks to prevent tax evasion and maintain transparency.

High-net-worth individual tax havens encompass a broad spectrum of tax advantages and financial services tailored to HNWIs. It is essential for bank regulators to understand the specific offerings of these havens, monitor compliance with international standards, and prevent any abuse or illegal activities.

Business tax havens attract entrepreneurs and corporations by offering low corporate tax rates, minimal bureaucracy, and favorable business environments. Bank regulators must ensure that these jurisdictions maintain a fair and transparent tax system, prevent tax evasion, and promote a level playing field for businesses.

Real estate investment tax havens provide tax incentives and advantages for HNWIs investing in real estate, stimulating economic growth and attracting foreign direct investment. Bank regulators should monitor these jurisdictions to prevent money laundering, ensure compliance with tax regulations, and promote transparency in real estate transactions.

Privacy-focused tax havens cater to individuals seeking to protect their financial privacy and personal information. These havens offer strict confidentiality laws, ensuring that personal financial information remains confidential. However, bank regulators must strike a balance between privacy and transparency to prevent money laundering, tax evasion, and illicit activities.

In conclusion, understanding the different niches within HNWI tax havens is crucial for bank regulators. By staying informed about offshore banking, digital nomad havens, retirement havens, cryptocurrency havens, asset protection havens, estate planning havens, business havens, real estate investment havens, and privacy-focused havens, regulators can effectively monitor compliance, prevent illicit activities, and maintain transparency in the global financial system.

Notable HNWI Tax Havens

In today's globalized world, high-net-worth individuals (HNWIs) are increasingly seeking tax-efficient jurisdictions to grow and protect their wealth. These individuals, along with businesses and digital nomads, are turning to offshore banking tax havens to take advantage of favorable tax regimes and other financial benefits. As bank regulators, it is essential to understand the dynamics of these tax havens and the implications they have on the global financial system. This subchapter aims to provide you with an overview of some notable HNWI tax havens across various niches, including offshore banking tax havens, digital nomad tax havens, retirement tax havens, cryptocurrency tax havens, asset protection tax havens, estate planning tax havens, high-net-worth individual tax havens, business tax havens, real estate investment tax havens, and privacy-focused tax havens.

Offshore banking tax havens are renowned for their low or zero tax rates, strict banking secrecy laws, and robust financial infrastructure. Notable jurisdictions in this category include Switzerland, the Cayman Islands, and Luxembourg. These havens attract HNWIs and businesses seeking to optimize their tax liabilities and protect their wealth from excessive taxation.

For digital nomads, who often work remotely and travel frequently, tax havens that offer favorable tax treatment are highly sought after. Locations like Estonia, Singapore, and Malta provide attractive tax incentives for foreign entrepreneurs and digital nomads, making them ideal destinations for this niche.

Retirement tax havens, such as Panama, Portugal, and Costa Rica, are popular among retirees looking for a comfortable lifestyle and tax advantages. These havens often offer attractive pension schemes, low tax rates, and a high standard of living.

Cryptocurrency tax havens have emerged as a new niche in recent years. Countries like Malta, Switzerland, and Bermuda have become havens for crypto investors, offering favorable tax treatment and regulatory frameworks that foster innovation in the cryptocurrency space.

Asset protection tax havens, like the Cook Islands, Belize, and Nevis, provide legal structures and trusts that safeguard assets from potential litigation and creditors. These jurisdictions offer robust asset protection laws and allow individuals to preserve their wealth for future generations.

Estate planning tax havens, such as Monaco, Liechtenstein, and Bermuda, provide attractive tax benefits for individuals looking to structure their estates efficiently. These jurisdictions offer favorable inheritance tax laws and facilitate the transfer of wealth to beneficiaries.

High-net-worth individuals often seek tax havens that cater specifically to their needs. Locations like Monaco, Andorra, and the Isle of Man offer exclusive services and amenities tailored to HNWIs, including private banking, luxury real estate, and high-end lifestyle options.

Business tax havens, including Ireland, Singapore, and Hong Kong, attract multinational corporations and entrepreneurs due to their favorable corporate tax rates, ease of doing business, and access to international markets.

Real estate investment tax havens, such as Dubai, Cyprus, and Portugal, provide attractive tax incentives and a thriving real estate market for investors seeking to diversify their portfolios and generate rental income.

Privacy-focused tax havens, like Switzerland, the British Virgin Islands, and Panama, offer strict banking secrecy laws and strict regulations on information sharing, ensuring the utmost privacy for individuals and businesses.

Understanding the nuances of these notable HNWI tax havens is crucial for bank regulators to effectively monitor and regulate offshore banking activities. By staying informed about the financial dynamics and specific characteristics of each tax haven, regulators can better ensure the integrity, stability, and transparency of the global financial system.

Monaco

Monaco: A Premier Offshore Banking Tax Haven

Monaco, the small sovereign city-state on the French Riviera, has long been renowned as a premier destination for offshore banking. With its advantageous tax system, political stability, and luxurious lifestyle, Monaco attracts a wide range of individuals and businesses seeking to optimize their financial strategies. This subchapter explores the unique aspects of Monaco as an offshore banking tax haven, catering specifically to the interests of bank regulators and various niche groups such as digital nomads, retirees, cryptocurrency enthusiasts, high-net-worth individuals, and more.

Bank regulators play a crucial role in overseeing the operations of offshore banks, ensuring compliance with international standards and preventing illicit activities. In Monaco, these regulators find a well-regulated and transparent financial environment, aligned with global banking norms. The government of Monaco has implemented robust anti-money laundering and know-your-customer frameworks, creating an environment conducive to responsible offshore banking.

For digital nomads seeking tax havens, Monaco offers an attractive proposition. With its favorable tax regime, including zero income tax on foreign-source income, digital nomads can enjoy the benefits of working remotely while minimizing their tax burdens. Additionally, Monaco's high-speed internet infrastructure, excellent healthcare system, and vibrant cultural scene make it an ideal base for the mobile workforce.

Retirees looking for a tax-efficient haven will find Monaco's retirement tax incentives highly appealing. With no tax on pensions or social security income, retirees can stretch their savings further and enjoy a comfortable lifestyle in the Mediterranean paradise. Furthermore,

Monaco's safe environment, excellent healthcare services, and favorable climate make it an ideal retirement destination.

Cryptocurrency enthusiasts and investors will find Monaco's friendly regulatory environment conducive to their activities. The principality has embraced blockchain technology and cryptocurrencies, providing a secure and supportive ecosystem for digital asset management. With its reputation as a tax haven, Monaco presents a unique opportunity for cryptocurrency investors to optimize their tax planning strategies.

High-net-worth individuals seeking asset protection and estate planning solutions will find Monaco an attractive jurisdiction. The country offers a wide range of wealth management services, including trust structures and inheritance planning, providing a secure and confidential environment for preserving and passing on wealth to future generations.

In conclusion, Monaco stands as a premier offshore banking tax haven, catering to the diverse needs of bank regulators and niche groups such as digital nomads, retirees, cryptocurrency enthusiasts, high-net-worth individuals, and more. With its favorable tax system, political stability, and luxurious lifestyle, Monaco remains a top choice for individuals and businesses seeking to navigate the offshore banking landscape.

Switzerland

Switzerland: A Haven for Offshore Banking and Tax Optimization

Switzerland has long been recognized as a premier destination for offshore banking and tax optimization. Renowned for its stability, privacy laws, and sophisticated financial system, this Alpine nation offers a multitude of advantages for individuals and businesses seeking to protect and grow their wealth.

Offshore banking tax havens:

Switzerland's reputation as an offshore banking tax haven is well-deserved. Its robust banking sector provides a wide range of services tailored to the needs of international clients. Swiss banks are known for their strict adherence to privacy, confidentiality, and security measures, ensuring that individuals and corporations can safeguard their assets and financial information.

Digital nomad tax havens:

For digital nomads, Switzerland offers an attractive tax regime. The country levies taxes based on residency rather than citizenship, allowing individuals with a nomadic lifestyle to benefit from favorable tax rates. Moreover, Switzerland's exceptional infrastructure, high-quality healthcare system, and stunning natural beauty make it an appealing location for remote workers seeking a high standard of living.

Retirement tax havens:

Switzerland's favorable tax laws, coupled with its political stability and exceptional healthcare system, make it an attractive destination for retirees. The country offers a range of retirement programs and tax incentives, ensuring that retirees can enjoy their golden years while optimizing their tax liabilities.

Cryptocurrency tax havens:

Switzerland has emerged as a leading jurisdiction for cryptocurrency enthusiasts. The country has embraced blockchain technology and digital currencies, providing a favorable regulatory environment for cryptocurrency businesses and investors. Switzerland's forward-thinking approach has attracted numerous blockchain startups and has positioned the country as a global hub for innovation in the crypto space.

Asset protection tax havens:

Switzerland's legal framework and strong rule of law make it an ideal destination for individuals seeking asset protection. The country's trust laws, combined with its sophisticated banking system, allow individuals to shield their assets from potential creditors and legal disputes. Swiss foundations and trusts provide a robust and reliable means of asset protection, ensuring peace of mind for high-net-worth individuals and families.

Estate planning tax havens:

Switzerland offers various estate planning opportunities for individuals looking to optimize their tax obligations. The country's inheritance laws, combined with its favorable tax regime, allow individuals to pass on their wealth to future generations while minimizing tax liabilities. Swiss private banks and wealth management firms specialize in providing tailored estate planning solutions to meet the unique needs of their clients.

High-net-worth individual tax havens:

Switzerland has long been a preferred destination for high-net-worth individuals seeking to optimize their tax burdens. The country offers a range of tax incentives, including lump-sum taxation, which allows wealthy individuals to pay a fixed annual tax amount based on their spending rather than their global income. This tax regime provides certainty and stability for high-net-worth individuals while fostering an environment conducive to wealth preservation and growth.

Business tax havens:

For businesses, Switzerland's advantageous tax system and stable economy make it an attractive location for international operations. The country offers low corporate tax rates, a favorable regulatory environment, and a highly skilled workforce. Swiss holding companies and special tax regimes, such as the mixed company regime, provide businesses with opportunities for tax optimization and efficient cross-border transactions.

Real estate investment tax havens:

Switzerland's real estate market is highly sought after by investors seeking stability and capital preservation. The country's strict regulations on foreign property ownership ensure that the market remains exclusive and resilient. Additionally, Switzerland's favorable tax laws incentivize real estate investment, allowing individuals and businesses to benefit from attractive tax rates and deductions.

Privacy-focused tax havens:

Switzerland's commitment to privacy and confidentiality has made it a preferred jurisdiction for individuals and businesses seeking to protect their financial information. The country's strong legal framework, stringent data protection laws, and robust banking secrecy provisions ensure that clients' privacy is safeguarded. Swiss banks and financial institutions adhere to strict due diligence procedures while providing a safe haven for those who prioritize privacy.

In conclusion, Switzerland's appeal as an offshore banking and tax optimization destination is undeniable. Its stable economy, sophisticated financial system, and commitment to privacy make it an attractive choice for a diverse range of individuals and businesses seeking to navigate the complexities of offshore banking and tax havens. From digital nomads to high-net-worth individuals and businesses, Switzerland offers a multitude of advantages for those looking to protect and grow their wealth.

Cayman Islands

Cayman Islands: A Haven for Offshore Banking

In the world of offshore banking, the Cayman Islands have long been regarded as one of the remaining safe tax havens. Situated in the Caribbean Sea, this British Overseas Territory offers a robust financial infrastructure, stringent regulation, and a favorable tax environment that attracts both individuals and corporations seeking to optimize their financial affairs.

Bank regulators play a critical role in ensuring the stability and integrity of the global financial system. Understanding the dynamics of offshore banking, particularly in safe tax havens like the Cayman Islands, is essential for effective regulation. This subchapter aims to provide bank regulators with a comprehensive overview of the Cayman Islands, shedding light on its regulatory framework, banking sector, and key considerations when engaging with this offshore jurisdiction.

Regulatory Framework: The Cayman Islands Monetary Authority (CIMA) serves as the primary regulatory body overseeing the jurisdiction's financial services industry. Bank regulators need to familiarize themselves with CIMA's role, functions, and licensing requirements, as well as its approach to anti-money laundering (AML) and combating the financing of terrorism (CFT) measures. Understanding the regulatory landscape is crucial for effective supervision and enforcement of financial regulations.

Banking Sector: The Cayman Islands' banking sector is renowned for its stability, confidentiality, and sophistication. Bank regulators should understand the different types of banks operating in the jurisdiction, including retail banks, private banks, and international banks. Exploring the services offered, capital requirements, and risk management practices of these banks will enable regulators to effectively oversee their operations and address any potential concerns.

Tax Environment: The Cayman Islands are known for their favorable tax environment, characterized by zero corporate income tax, no capital gains tax, and no withholding tax on dividends or interest. Bank regulators need to be aware of the implications of this tax regime, including the potential for tax evasion and money laundering. Collaborating with tax authorities and other regulatory bodies becomes crucial to ensure compliance and transparency in the global financial system.

Key Considerations: This subchapter also highlights some key considerations for bank regulators when engaging with the Cayman Islands. These include understanding the jurisdiction's relationship with international organizations and initiatives, such as the Financial Action Task Force (FATF) and the Organisation for Economic Co-operation and Development (OECD). Additionally, regulators must be aware of recent developments, such as economic substance requirements, and their impact on offshore banking activities.

In conclusion, the Cayman Islands' status as one of the world's remaining safe tax havens makes it a critical jurisdiction for bank regulators to understand. By delving into the regulatory framework, banking sector, tax environment, and key considerations, regulators can navigate the complexities of offshore banking in this jurisdiction and fulfill their role in maintaining the integrity of the global financial system.

Bahamas

Bahamas: A Premier Offshore Banking and Tax Haven

The Bahamas has long been recognized as one of the world's premier offshore banking and tax havens, offering a multitude of benefits to individuals and businesses seeking financial privacy, asset protection, and tax optimization. As bank regulators, it is crucial to understand the key features and opportunities that the Bahamas presents within the realm of offshore banking.

Offshore banking tax havens have become increasingly popular among high-net-worth individuals, digital nomads, and retirees seeking to optimize their financial affairs. The Bahamas, with its stable political environment, robust financial infrastructure, and favorable tax regime, is an ideal destination for those looking to safeguard their wealth and minimize their tax liabilities.

One of the major advantages of banking in the Bahamas is the absence of personal income tax, capital gains tax, and inheritance tax. This attractive tax environment allows individuals and businesses to legally reduce their tax burdens, facilitating wealth preservation and growth. Additionally, the Bahamas offers a range of tax incentives for businesses, making it an appealing destination for entrepreneurs and investors.

For digital nomads and individuals earning income from remote work or online businesses, the Bahamas provides an excellent opportunity to take advantage of its tax neutrality. By establishing residency in the Bahamas, digital nomads can enjoy a tax-free income while enjoying the country's beautiful landscapes and warm climate.

Moreover, the Bahamas has emerged as a cryptocurrency tax haven, attracting investors and businesses involved in the digital currency space. The government has implemented progressive regulations that create a supportive environment for cryptocurrency transactions and blockchain-based businesses. This has positioned the Bahamas as a hub for cryptocurrency enthusiasts seeking privacy, security, and favorable tax treatment.

In addition to its tax benefits, the Bahamas offers a high level of asset protection and privacy. Its strong legal framework safeguards individuals and businesses against frivolous lawsuits, ensuring their assets remain secure. The country's strict confidentiality laws further enhance privacy and protect sensitive financial information.

Furthermore, the Bahamas is an ideal jurisdiction for estate planning, offering various trust structures and estate planning tools. Individuals can establish trusts to protect and manage their assets, ensuring a smooth transfer of wealth to future generations while mitigating tax obligations.

For those interested in real estate investment, the Bahamas provides an array of opportunities. Its stable and growing real estate market, coupled with attractive tax breaks, makes it an appealing option for investors seeking to diversify their portfolios.

Bank regulators must be cognizant of the unique advantages and challenges that arise from offshore banking in the Bahamas. It is imperative to strike a balance between ensuring compliance with international banking standards and enabling the growth and development of the country's offshore financial sector.

In conclusion, the Bahamas offers a multitude of advantages for individuals and businesses seeking offshore banking and tax havens. With its favorable tax regime, robust financial infrastructure, and commitment to privacy and asset protection, the Bahamas remains a prominent destination for high-net-worth individuals, digital nomads, retirees, cryptocurrency enthusiasts, and others. Bank regulators must stay abreast of the evolving landscape of offshore banking in the Bahamas to effectively navigate and regulate this thriving sector.

Luxembourg

Luxembourg: A Premier Offshore Banking and Tax Haven

Introduction:

Luxembourg holds a prominent position in the world of offshore banking and tax havens, offering a range of advantages for individuals and businesses alike. This subchapter explores the unique features and benefits that make Luxembourg an attractive destination for various niches within the offshore banking industry, including digital nomads, retirees, cryptocurrency enthusiasts, high-net-worth individuals, and more.

1. Offshore Banking Tax Haven:

Luxembourg's favorable tax regime and robust financial infrastructure make it an ideal location for offshore banking. With its extensive network of double tax treaties, low withholding taxes, and attractive tax incentives, this European nation provides a secure and stable environment for both personal and corporate banking needs.

2. Digital Nomad Tax Haven:

For digital nomads seeking a tax-efficient jurisdiction, Luxembourg offers an appealing solution. With its flexible residency requirements, low personal income tax rates, and vibrant digital ecosystem, it provides an ideal base for location-independent professionals looking to optimize their tax obligations while enjoying a high standard of living.

3. Retirement Tax Haven:

Luxembourg's well-developed retirement planning options, including private pension funds and favorable tax treatment for retirees, make it an excellent choice for those seeking a secure and tax-efficient retirement destination. The country's stable economy, excellent healthcare system, and high quality of life further enhance its appeal for retirees.

4. Cryptocurrency Tax Haven:

As a leading hub for fintech and blockchain innovation, Luxembourg has emerged as a favorable jurisdiction for cryptocurrency enthusiasts.

Its clear regulatory framework, favorable tax treatment for cryptocurrencies, and supportive government initiatives make it an attractive destination for individuals and businesses operating in the digital asset space.

5. Asset Protection and Estate Planning Tax Haven:

Luxembourg's strong legal framework and sophisticated wealth management services make it an ideal jurisdiction for asset protection and estate planning. Its trust and foundation structures, combined with favorable tax treatment for wealth transfers, provide individuals and families with a secure and efficient means of preserving and passing on their assets.

6. High-net-worth Individual Tax Haven:

Luxembourg's reputation as a high-net-worth individual tax haven is well-deserved. Its attractive tax regime, wealth management expertise, and extensive range of financial services cater specifically to the needs of affluent individuals looking to optimize their tax burden while benefiting from a secure and prestigious banking environment.

7. Business and Real Estate Investment Tax Haven:

Luxembourg's business-friendly environment, strategic location, and access to the European market make it an ideal destination for international businesses and real estate investors. With its favorable corporate tax rates, efficient company formation process, and extensive network of double tax treaties, Luxembourg offers a stable and advantageous platform for global business operations.

8. Privacy-focused Tax Haven:

For those seeking privacy and confidentiality, Luxembourg's strong data protection laws and commitment to privacy make it an attractive choice. With strict regulations on information sharing and a long-standing tradition of financial secrecy, Luxembourg provides individuals and businesses with a high level of privacy and discretion.

Conclusion:

Luxembourg's reputation as a premier offshore banking and tax haven is well-founded. Its favorable tax regime, robust financial infrastructure, and commitment to privacy make it an attractive destination for a wide range of individuals and businesses within the offshore banking industry. Whether you are a digital nomad, retiree, cryptocurrency enthusiast, high-net-worth individual, or business owner, Luxembourg offers a secure and advantageous environment to meet your offshore banking needs.

Wealth Management and Tax Planning for HNWIs in Tax Havens

As bank regulators, it is crucial to understand the intricacies of wealth management and tax planning for high-net-worth individuals (HNWIs) in tax havens. Tax havens have long been popular among various niches, including offshore banking, digital nomads, retirees, cryptocurrency enthusiasts, asset protectors, estate planners, high-net-worth individuals, business owners, real estate investors, and those seeking privacy-focused solutions. This subchapter aims to provide you with insights into the unique challenges and opportunities that arise in these specific niches.

Tax havens offer a range of advantages for HNWIs, including low or zero tax rates, asset protection, and financial privacy. However, navigating the complex landscape of tax planning and wealth management in these jurisdictions requires careful consideration and expertise.

For offshore banking tax havens, it is essential to understand the regulatory framework and the potential risks associated with offshore accounts. As bank regulators, your role is to ensure the integrity of the financial system while allowing for legitimate offshore banking activities.

Digital nomad tax havens present a unique set of challenges due to the transient nature of these individuals. Tax planning for digital nomads requires a thorough understanding of their income sources, residency requirements, and the tax implications of working remotely across different jurisdictions.

Retirement tax havens attract individuals seeking to maximize their retirement income and minimize tax obligations. Understanding the specific retirement schemes, tax incentives, and estate planning opportunities available in these jurisdictions is crucial for effective regulation.

Cryptocurrency tax havens have emerged as a niche within tax havens, catering to individuals and businesses dealing with digital assets. The regulatory landscape for cryptocurrencies is rapidly evolving, and it is important to stay abreast of new developments to ensure a well-regulated and secure environment.

Asset protection tax havens appeal to individuals seeking to shield their wealth from potential legal threats. As bank regulators, it is essential to strike a balance between providing asset protection solutions and preventing illicit activities such as money laundering or tax evasion.

Estate planning tax havens offer a range of opportunities for individuals looking to secure and preserve their wealth for future generations. Understanding the legal frameworks, trusts, and tax implications of estate planning in these jurisdictions is essential for effective regulation.

High-net-worth individual tax havens cater specifically to individuals with substantial wealth. These jurisdictions often offer tailor-made wealth management solutions, including investment opportunities, tax planning strategies, and financial privacy.

Business tax havens attract entrepreneurs and corporations seeking favorable tax environments and a robust business ecosystem. As bank regulators, it is crucial to ensure compliance with international tax standards and prevent abusive practices.

Real estate investment tax havens offer attractive opportunities for individuals looking to invest in properties abroad. Understanding the tax implications, legal frameworks, and potential risks associated with real estate investments is crucial for effective regulation.

Privacy-focused tax havens cater to individuals seeking financial privacy and confidentiality. Striking a balance between privacy rights and preventing illicit activities is a key challenge for bank regulators in these jurisdictions.

In conclusion, wealth management and tax planning for HNWIs in tax havens require a deep understanding of the specific niches within offshore banking. As bank regulators, it is crucial to ensure the integrity of the financial system while facilitating legitimate wealth management activities. By staying informed about the unique challenges and opportunities in these niches, you can effectively regulate and oversee tax havens to maintain a secure and well-regulated environment for all stakeholders involved.

Private Banking Services

Private banking services play a crucial role in the offshore banking industry, catering to a diverse range of clients seeking specialized financial solutions. This subchapter will delve into the intricacies of private banking services and their significance in the realm of offshore banking, addressing the specific needs and requirements of various niche markets such as offshore banking tax havens, digital nomad tax havens, retirement tax havens, cryptocurrency tax havens, asset protection tax havens, estate planning tax havens, high-net-worth individual tax havens, business tax havens, real estate investment tax havens, and privacy-focused tax havens.

Private banking services are tailored to high-net-worth individuals, providing them with personalized financial advice and a wide array of sophisticated investment options. In offshore banking tax havens, private banking services aim to optimize tax efficiency by utilizing legal strategies and structures, ensuring clients' assets are protected while minimizing their tax burdens.

For digital nomad tax havens, private banking services offer innovative solutions to manage and invest income generated from remote work. These services enable digital nomads to maintain financial stability, benefit from tax advantages, and access a range of international investment opportunities.

Retirement tax havens present unique challenges and opportunities. Private banking services in these jurisdictions focus on asset preservation, wealth management, and long-term financial planning to ensure a comfortable retirement for clients.

The emergence of cryptocurrencies has led to the creation of cryptocurrency tax havens. Private banking services in these jurisdictions offer secure storage, investment solutions, and guidance on navigating the complex regulatory landscape surrounding digital assets.

Asset protection tax havens provide a safe haven for individuals seeking to safeguard their wealth from legal disputes, political instability, or economic uncertainty. Private banking services in these jurisdictions offer comprehensive asset protection strategies, including trust structures and offshore company formations.

Estate planning tax havens cater to clients looking to efficiently pass on their wealth to future generations. Private banking services in these jurisdictions provide expertise in estate planning, trust administration, and inheritance tax optimization.

High-net-worth individual tax havens offer exclusive private banking services to ultra-wealthy clients, focusing on personalized investment strategies, access to exclusive investment opportunities, and comprehensive wealth management solutions.

Business tax havens attract companies seeking favorable tax regimes and a business-friendly environment. Private banking services in these jurisdictions assist businesses in managing their finances, optimizing tax efficiency, and facilitating international transactions.

Real estate investment tax havens offer private banking services tailored to investors interested in lucrative real estate opportunities. These services include property financing, portfolio diversification, and expert advice on local real estate markets.

Finally, privacy-focused tax havens cater to individuals who value their financial privacy. Private banking services in these jurisdictions prioritize client confidentiality, offering anonymous banking solutions, offshore trusts, and discreet asset management.

In summary, private banking services in offshore banking tax havens serve a diverse range of niche markets, providing tailored solutions to meet the specific needs of clients. These services encompass investment advice, wealth management, tax optimization, asset protection, estate planning, and specialized solutions for high-net-worth individuals, businesses, digital nomads, retirees, cryptocurrency enthusiasts, real estate investors, and those seeking financial privacy.

Investment Structures

In today's globalized economy, offshore banking has become a popular avenue for individuals and businesses to optimize their financial strategies. As bank regulators, it is crucial to understand the various investment structures that are commonly used in offshore banking tax havens. This subchapter aims to provide you with an overview of different investment structures and their implications for the niches of offshore banking tax havens, including digital nomad tax havens, retirement tax havens, cryptocurrency tax havens, asset protection tax havens, estate planning tax havens, high-net-worth individual tax havens, business tax havens, real estate investment tax havens, and privacy-focused tax havens.

One of the primary investment structures utilized in offshore banking tax havens is the establishment of offshore companies and trusts. Offshore companies offer a range of benefits, such as tax optimization, asset protection, and increased privacy. These structures are particularly attractive to digital nomads, who can leverage the flexibility of offshore companies to manage their global income and assets efficiently.

For individuals planning their retirement, offshore pension schemes provide a compelling option. These structures offer tax advantages, investment diversification, and greater control over retirement funds. Bank regulators need to stay informed about the regulations and safeguards in place to ensure the integrity of these retirement tax havens.

Cryptocurrency tax havens are emerging as a popular choice for investors seeking to capitalize on the growing digital currency market. These havens offer a favorable regulatory environment, low tax rates, and sophisticated infrastructure for cryptocurrency transactions. Regulators should closely monitor these jurisdictions to prevent money laundering and other illicit activities.

Asset protection structures, such as offshore trusts and foundations, are vital for safeguarding wealth against potential risks. These structures are particularly relevant for high-net-worth individuals seeking to shield their assets from legal claims, creditors, and inheritance taxes. Bank regulators must ensure that these structures are not misused for illicit purposes.

Estate planning tax havens provide individuals with the opportunity to efficiently manage their inheritance and succession plans. By utilizing offshore trusts and foundations, individuals can minimize estate taxes, maintain privacy, and ensure the smooth transfer of assets to future generations.

Business tax havens attract companies seeking favorable tax regimes, flexible regulatory frameworks, and increased privacy for their operations. Bank regulators play a critical role in overseeing these jurisdictions to prevent money laundering, tax evasion, and other illicit activities.

Real estate investment tax havens offer attractive opportunities for investors looking to diversify their portfolios. These havens provide tax benefits, a stable legal environment, and potential capital appreciation. Regulators should ensure that real estate transactions in these jurisdictions are transparent and adhere to anti-money laundering regulations.

Privacy-focused tax havens cater to individuals and businesses looking for enhanced financial privacy and confidentiality. While privacy is an important aspect of offshore banking, regulators must strike a balance between privacy and preventing illegal activities, such as money laundering.

Understanding the various investment structures in offshore banking tax havens is crucial for bank regulators to effectively oversee these jurisdictions. By staying informed and vigilant, regulators can ensure the integrity and transparency of offshore banking operations while mitigating the risks associated with tax evasion, money laundering, and other illicit activities.

Tax Optimization Strategies

In today's globalized economy, tax optimization strategies play a crucial role in the functioning of offshore banking and tax havens. As bank regulators, it is essential to have a comprehensive understanding of these strategies to ensure the smooth operation of offshore banking institutions. This subchapter will delve into various tax optimization strategies employed in different niches of offshore banking, catering to the needs of digital nomads, retirees, cryptocurrency enthusiasts, high-net-worth individuals, and more.

1. Offshore Banking Tax Havens:

Offshore banking tax havens offer favorable tax regimes to attract investors and businesses. Understanding the legal framework, tax incentives, and compliance requirements of these jurisdictions is crucial for bank regulators to effectively oversee the operations and mitigate risks associated with tax evasion or money laundering.

2. Digital Nomad Tax Havens:

Digital nomads, who work remotely while traveling, require tax-friendly jurisdictions that cater to their unique needs. Exploring tax havens that offer special visa programs and tax benefits for digital nomads can help regulators understand the challenges and opportunities associated with this emerging trend.

3. Retirement Tax Havens:

Retirement tax havens provide attractive tax incentives for retirees seeking a peaceful and financially stable lifestyle. Regulators need to be aware of the retirement-specific tax benefits and ensure compliance with relevant regulations to safeguard retirees' interests.

4. Cryptocurrency Tax Havens:

The rise of cryptocurrencies has given birth to tax havens specifically tailored to crypto enthusiasts. Understanding the tax implications, regulatory frameworks, and security measures surrounding cryptocurrency transactions is indispensable for regulators overseeing these niche markets.

5. Asset Protection Tax Havens:

Bank regulators must comprehend the asset protection strategies employed in tax havens to safeguard individuals' wealth from potential risks. This includes understanding trust structures, offshore company formations, and legal mechanisms employed in asset protection tax havens.

6. Estate Planning Tax Havens:

Estate planning tax havens offer unique advantages for individuals seeking to optimize their wealth transfer and inheritance strategies. Familiarizing themselves with estate planning tools, such as trusts and foundations, will enable regulators to effectively oversee these jurisdictions.

7. High-Net-Worth Individual Tax Havens:

High-net-worth individuals often seek tax havens that provide a favorable environment for wealth management, investment opportunities, and tax optimization. Regulators should understand the intricacies of catering to this niche segment while ensuring compliance with anti-money laundering and tax transparency regulations.

8. Business Tax Havens:

Bank regulators need to stay updated on tax optimization strategies employed by businesses in tax havens. This includes understanding the benefits of offshore company formations, double tax treaties, and transfer pricing mechanisms while ensuring compliance with international tax standards.

9. Real Estate Investment Tax Havens:

Tax havens that offer attractive tax incentives for real estate investments require regulators to be well-versed in real estate taxation laws, property ownership structures, and compliance requirements to ensure transparency and prevent illicit activities.

10. Privacy-Focused Tax Havens:

Privacy-focused tax havens emphasize confidentiality and data protection. Regulators must understand the balance between privacy rights, preventing financial crimes, and ensuring tax transparency to effectively supervise these jurisdictions.

By comprehending the tax optimization strategies employed in various niches of offshore banking, bank regulators can effectively oversee and regulate these jurisdictions. This understanding will enable regulators to ensure compliance, prevent financial crimes, and maintain the integrity and stability of offshore banking institutions.

Chapter 9: Business Tax Havens

Overview of Business Tax

In today's globalized economy, businesses often seek opportunities beyond their home countries to optimize their financial operations. One way they achieve this is through offshore banking in tax havens. This subchapter provides an overview of business tax in such jurisdictions and explores its implications for bank regulators.

Offshore banking tax havens offer businesses favorable tax regimes, allowing them to minimize their tax liabilities legally. These jurisdictions typically have low or no corporate income tax, capital gains tax, or value-added tax. By establishing their operations in these tax havens, businesses can maximize their profits and reinvest in growth initiatives.

For bank regulators overseeing offshore banking tax havens, understanding the nuances of business tax is essential. They must ensure that the tax policies of these jurisdictions are fair, transparent, and compliant with international standards. Regulators play a crucial role in balancing the interests of businesses and the broader financial system.

Digital nomad tax havens, retirement tax havens, cryptocurrency tax havens, asset protection tax havens, estate planning tax havens, high-net-worth individual tax havens, and real estate investment tax havens are all subsets of business tax havens. Each of these niches has specific tax implications that regulators need to be aware of to effectively regulate offshore banking activities.

For instance, digital nomads often leverage tax havens to manage their tax liabilities while working remotely. Regulators must ensure that these individuals comply with tax obligations both in their home countries and in the tax havens they operate from.

Cryptocurrency tax havens have emerged as a new frontier in the digital economy. Regulators need to stay abreast of developments in this space to prevent money laundering, illicit activities, and tax evasion. Effective regulation can strike a balance between facilitating innovation and safeguarding the integrity of the financial system.

Bank regulators also need to be cognizant of the potential risks associated with business tax havens. While these jurisdictions provide opportunities for legitimate businesses, they can also attract illicit financial flows and tax evasion. Regulators must implement robust anti-money laundering and counter-terrorism financing measures to prevent abuse of these tax havens.

In conclusion, an overview of business tax in offshore banking tax havens is crucial for bank regulators. By understanding the intricacies of different tax niches, regulators can ensure fair and transparent tax policies, mitigate risks associated with tax evasion, and strike a balance between facilitating legitimate business activities and safeguarding the financial system.